ELLAVATE

Elevate your life after toxic love

7 Steps on how I *ditched* dating drama and relationship shitshows to elevate my entire life

By Ann-Kathrin Petersen

Copyright © 2025

All Rights Reserved

Acknowledgements

To my mum and stepdad—thank you from the depths of my heart. During my journey of healing and rediscovering myself, you were my rock. You gave me the space and support I needed to find my path; you encouraged me to go after my dreams, even when my goals seemed far-fetched. Your love and daily support gave me the strength to build a life I now love!

To my dear friends Katka, Nathalie, and Gyde—your unwavering belief in me and unconditional love mean the world. You are there when I need to find my light again and keep reminding me of my worth. Thank you for accepting and loving me for who I am.

Thank you to Debs—you were the spark that ignited my healing.

Thank you to my dear colleagues from the T.P.I. who supported and guided me through my journey of self-discovery. I feel seen, heard, understood, appreciated, and accepted for being me. Believing in my potential and going after my dreams became a reality thanks to you!

Your guidance and support gave me the courage to take the first brave steps toward transformation. You helped me begin the process of creating the life I was meant to live, and for that, I am forever grateful.

To all of you, thank you for being part of my journey. This book wouldn't exist without your love and support.

Dedication

To Ella - The Love of my Life!

You showed me how to keep a broken heart open, be strong, and stand up for a happy life!

About the Author

Ann-Kathrin Petersen is a dedicated mindset coach, trauma educator, and EFT practitioner committed to guiding individuals toward personal elevation. Her extensive experience spans working with women in various life stages, including those in women's shelters and refugee camps, as well as professional athletes, assisting them in overcoming inner blocks and healing from traumatic experiences. Drawing from her own journey through abusive relationships and the pursuit of external validation, Ann-Kathrin transformed her life by breaking free from toxic love and codependency. This personal evolution, combined with her professional expertise, inspired her to create "ELLAVATE," a mission-driven initiative aimed at combating domestic violence and abuse and empowering women to rebuild their lives post-abuse.

Through her work, Ann-Kathrin has facilitated profound transformations, helping women worldwide cultivate self-love, develop conscious dating habits, build healthy relationships, and lead fulfilling lives. Her vision is to make a significant contribution to the elimination of domestic violence, offering guidance to those seeking to break free from codependency and embrace authentic confidence.

Table of Contents:

Introduction: 1
    My Vision and Hope – Why This Book Is So Important To Me! ... 4
    Love Letter - My Wish to YOU! 7
    Story of Ellavate: 10
Welcome To Team Ellavate, Babe! 13
    In Pursuit of You: 15
Step 1 – Get Out of the (Shitty) Relationship: 18
    The Two Relationships You Must Walk Away From: 23
        Toxic vs. Abusive Relationships: 24
        Stop Searching for Excuses—Start Searching for Your Power: 25
        Breaking the Cycle: 25
        The Cycle of Abuse: 26
        How to Break the Cycle: 27
        If Someone You Love Is in an Abusive Relationship: 28
    My Story—and the Scars That Still Speak: 31
        Understanding the Love-Bombing Phase and Letting Go: 32
        Realizing this shifted my perspective: 33
        Most Abusers Use These Stages: 34
        Kids and Abuse: 40
        Leaving Isn't Just for You. It's for Them: 41
        You Are Their Safe Place: 41
    Things I Did While Being in Toxic Relationships: 42
    Trauma Bonding: 45
    Involving the Police? 46
    Know Your Rights: 47

  When the Relationship Isn't Dangerous—Just *Meh:* 48
  The 10/90 Rule: 50
Step 2 – Dating Sabbatical: 51
  Why Take a Dating Sabbatical? 51
  No More "Backups": 53
  How to Handle Triggers and Emotions: 54
  The Ellavate Challenge: 56
Step 3 – The Ellavate Challenge: 58
  Your Daily Practices: 59
  It's time to come back to yourself. It's time to Ellavate: 61
    How to Start: 61
    1. Meditation: 61
    2. Morning Pages: 63
    3. EFT Tapping: 65
    4. Workout – Move Your Body, Elevate Your Life: 74
    5. Cold Shower – Embrace Discomfort, Build Resilience: ... 78
    6. Stick to an Eating Plan – Nourish to Flourish 82
    7. Drink Water – A Gallon a Day! 84
    8. The Vortex Game 87
    9. Read 10 Pages a Day: 93
    10. Taking Action Toward Your Dreams: 94
  Add-Ons: Make the Challenge Yours: 96
  The Magical Morning Practice (MMP): 98
  Acupuncture – NADA: 100
  Why the Ellavate Challenge Is So Important: 101
Step 4 – Love Yourself: 103
  The Uncomfortable Journey to Self-Love! 104

- Raising Your Standards through Self-Love! 105
- The Love Bucket: 106
  - How Do You Repair the Love Bucket? 107
  - Exercise - Take a Moment for You: 108
- Mirror Work: 109
  - What Is Mirror Work? 109
  - Mirror Work + Tapping = Magic: 112
  - For Moms, Kids, and Healing Hearts: 113
- Self-Love vs. Self-Care: 115
- Self-love and Confidence: 116
- Practical Ways to Love Yourself: 118

Step 5: Coming Home (To Yourself): 144
- Self-Discovery Through Different Methods: 145
- The Subconscious Mind – Running on Autopilot: 146
  - Exercise 148
- Me, Myself, and I: 149
  - Inner Child: 150
  - The Inner Teenager: 151
  - The Ego: 151
  - The Higher Self: 151
  - Reclaiming Your Truth: 152
- ATTACHMENT VS. LOVE: 154
- ATTACHMENT STYLES: THE BLUEPRINT OF HOW YOU LOVE: 156
- SECURE ATTACHMENT: THE "MYTHICAL UNICORN": 156
- ANXIOUS ATTACHMENT: MY STORY, MY STRUGGLE: . 157
- AVOIDANT ATTACHMENT: THE MEN I DATED (AGAIN AND AGAIN): 157

- DISORGANIZED ATTACHMENT: THE LOVE–PANIC SPIRAL: ... 158
- WHEN LOVE BECOMES AN ADDICTION: CODEPENDENCY AND THE ROOTS OF REPEATING RELATIONSHIP PAIN: ... 158
- LOVE AS A BATTLEFIELD: ... 159
- LETTING GO OF THE VICTIM STORY: ... 160
- HEALING CODEPENDENCY: THE REAL WORK: ... 160
  - From Self-Loathing to Self-Love: ... 162
  - Final Thoughts: This Ends With You ... 163
  - What is the Imago Blueprint? ... 163
  - The Imago Blueprint Exercise: Rewriting Your Type: ... 164
  - Write What You Needed as a Child: ... 165
  - Remember the Good: ... 166
  - Uncover Childhood Frustrations and Your Responses: ... 166
  - Build Your Love Blueprint: ... 168
  - Rewrite Your Blueprint: ... 168
  - Visualization: Giving It Back ... 169
  - A Gentle Reminder: ... 170
  - Trusting Yourself: ... 170
  - Healing Your Trauma — The Way Back Home to Yourself: ... 173
- Step 6 – Build Your Own Life: ... 176
  - Your Physical Home — Building the Ground Beneath Your Feet: ... 177
  - From Self-Discovery to Self-Construction: ... 178
  - Daring to Dream (Again): ... 179
  - Manifestation: Making Your Dreams Real: ... 181
    - Purpose: ... 182
    - Less Stress, More Freedom: ... 183

Self-Worth: 184
Becoming the Queen of Your Queendom: 184
A Transition into Love — The Queen Meets the King: 186
Step 7 – Dating: 188
Phase Two – The Conscious Dating Experience: 189
Afterthought: You Are the Blueprint 191
The Ellavate Journal: Prompts for Self-Awareness, Healing & Expansion: 192
1. Morning Grounding: Start With Intention: 192
2. Self-Discovery & Emotional Awareness: 192
3. Inner Child & Emotional Roots: 192
4. Attachment Style & Codependency: 193
5. Love Blueprint (Imago Work): 193
6. Reclaiming Your Power: 194
7. Forgiveness & Compassion: 194
8. Dating Sabbatical & Solo Clarity: 194
9. Relationship Clarity: 195
10. Self-Love & Mirror Work: 195
11. Healing Your Heart: The Love Bucket: 195
12. Building Your Own Life: 196
13. Morning & Evening Check-Ins (Daily Practice) 196

Introduction:

This book is written for you to get a cup of tea, sit back, and imagine me talking to you in one of your favourite places about how I elevated from toxic love, dating drama, and losing myself in the midst of it, into a more confident, happy version of myself.

Imagine us sitting in front of each other and you asking me, *"What did you do to get out of abuse and overcome dating drama? How could you go back on dates after everything you have been through? Can you share with me what you learned and how you did it?"*

I am sharing how I elevated my life during a time I didn't think I would survive. Life after abuse did not seem possible for me. What I found helpful transformed not only my love but my entire life.

First and foremost: Congratulations on wanting to elevate too! Elevating is not for the faint-hearted — it is for those of us ready to get more out of life and take the reins in our own hands.

Perhaps you once waited for Prince Charming on his white horse (or, as the joke goes, in his *black Porsche*) to come along and rescue you, only to realise they never truly rescued you. In fact, life only became more difficult with the "wannabe prince" in your life. You came to see you were being treated as a doormat, used, and left heartbroken.

Now it is time to leave behind this princess mindset, ditch the drama, and raise your standards to those of a Queen! You might still hope for 'The Right One' to make your life feel like a honeymoon and bring you a "happy ending". But this book challenges those ideas, inviting you to join *Team Ellavate*.

Take a good look in the mirror and see that the only person who can rescue you is **YOU**.

By picking up this book, you have chosen to elevate!
You chose to step up in life!
You chose to ditch love, relationship, and dating drama!
You chose YOU!
So, take a deep breath and thank yourself!

If dating is new to you, congratulations on starting the journey differently than I did — woke, aware, confident, and knowing that healthy, balanced love that enriches your life is the only way to go. That is my wish for you.

This book is written from a woman's perspective, most likely for other women dating men. But no matter your gender or preference, you can adapt the message to your own life. These are my experiences and my answers to the question I am so often asked: "How did you elevate?"

There are many paths to a better life, and many tools that can help you elevate. Here, I am sharing what worked for me.

I am not a licensed therapist, but I have gained insight during and after my healing, supported by professional knowledge along the way.

This book comes from my perspective as a woman with a story to tell — a story of how abuse and unhealthy relationships once held me hostage, kept me from shining my light, and stopped me from elevating.

It is the journey of moving from self-loathing to self-love, from relying on men to save me (and losing myself in the process) to finally saving myself and creating a life I truly love.

I share this journey to guide and inspire you to choose your own path — and elevate too.

My Vision and Hope – Why This Book Is So Important To Me!

As a victim of domestic violence, I know what it feels like to be in unhealthy love — to feel trapped in a situation that is not good for you. I know what it is to stay in an unpleasant, sometimes even dangerous, place filled with shame, guilt, and the overwhelming fear of how to escape.

I know what it feels like to pretend everything is fine because you don't know how to ask for help. I have been too deep in it, not knowing a way out, to the point where I almost took my own life. I know the dizzying cycle of abuse, when life spins so fast you truly believe there is no escape.

But I also worked my way out — and have since worked with many women who faced the same struggles.

I want to end domestic violence. I want to be part of the group of people who help create healthy love in this world.

My belief is that this is only possible if we work on our inner selves. Insecurities, unhealthy attachment styles, and the habit of allowing our boundaries to be crossed — all rooted in childhood experiences and societal norms — are major reasons why we end up in relationships marked by aggression.

Estimates published by the WHO indicate that globally, about 1 in 3 women (30%) have been subjected to physical and/or sexual intimate partner violence in their lifetime (WHO, 2024).

Every 10 minutes, one woman is killed by an intimate or ex-partner (The Hotline, 2023).

In the United States, 1 in 4 women have reported experiencing severe physical violence by an intimate partner (The Hotline, 2023).

Intimate partner violence alone affects more than 12 million people every year.

These numbers are far too high — and remember, these are only the official ones. Most cases go unreported. Change must happen, and one vital step is to begin by looking within ourselves.

While ending domestic violence is a core part of my mission, I am equally driven to explore what healthy, fulfilling love looks like. It is not only about escaping abuse — it is also about refusing to settle for relationships that feel safe but are ultimately unfulfilling. Relationships where love is missing, growth has stalled, and both partners quietly yearn for more.

People staying in unhappy situations is a waste of potential, a waste of life, and a waste of the joy we could experience in the time we have. Relationships do not need to be toxic or abusive to drain you of your energy. They do not need to be openly aggressive for us to recognise the need for change.

Strangely, I see my abusive relationships as a blessing — because they forced me to leave. For me, it was life or death. Being pushed to that edge made me rethink love and rebuild my life differently.

As a coach working with women on confidence and relationships, I see the same unhappiness play out again and again. It hurts to witness so much suffering caused by unhealthy love. This is why I share my own journey — from abuse and unhappiness to a life without drama and stress.

What I have learnt has supported women at many stages of their love lives: those wanting to break unhealthy patterns, those struggling to move on from painful breakups, and even teenage girls just starting to date. My approach begins with the belief that dating drama arises when something inside us keeps pulling us towards partners who are not good for us. My work is about changing that pattern.

Of course, abusive people should be held accountable, and I am grateful for the times when police stepped in to protect me. But prevention matters most. I want to help women create change within themselves so they do not choose the wrong person in the first place.

My vision is that these ideas and my learnings will contribute to change in the world — especially when mothers heal and stop passing these patterns on to the next generation.

Love Letter - My Wish to YOU!

My dear darling,

  If you are reading this, trust me, I know you are hurting. Your heart feels shattered, and you are not sure how to hold it. Maybe you feel numb. Maybe you feel everything all at once. Maybe you are wondering how something that once felt like love could leave you feeling so lost, so betrayed, so deeply alone.

  I want you to know—I see you.

  I see the pain you don't talk about. The way you question yourself in the quiet hours. The moments you wonder if it was your fault, if you stayed too long, if you should have known better. The way you carry the weight of someone else's harm and wear it like it's yours to bear. I see the strength it takes just to get out of bed some days, to go through the motions when your soul is aching.

  I know, because I have been there too. I have lived through the heartbreak that shatters your sense of self. I have felt the confusion, the shame, and the slow erosion of self-worth in the name of "love." I know how it feels to be gaslit until you no longer trust your own memories, to beg for breadcrumbs and still be left starving, to lose pieces of yourself while trying to be enough for someone who never saw your light.

  Let me tell you something you may not believe just yet: you are not broken. You are not to blame. You are not too much, and you are not alone. What happened to you does not define you.

The pain you carry is not a reflection of your value — it's a reflection of someone else's inability to meet you with care, truth, and respect.

Even now, in the wreckage, something sacred remains: **YOU**.

Here is what I need you to know: you will rise. Maybe not today. Maybe not all at once. But one breath, one step, one small act of self-kindness at a time — you will come home to yourself.

This time, you won't abandon who you are to be loved. You will rebuild from the truth. From your own centre. From a place where you are no longer trying to be chosen — because, my love, you choose you.

You are allowed to take your time. To cry. To be angry. To feel like you are crumbling. Healing is not linear — it's messy, holy, and entirely your own. But please, don't stay in the rubble. Don't make a home out of the heartbreak. This pain is a passage, not a destination. There is life after this. Not just any life, but one that feels free, aligned, full of peace, full of you.

One day, the heaviness in your chest will lift. One day, you will smile again, and it won't feel forced. One day, your nervous system will feel safe. Your heart will soften. You will look in the mirror and see a whole woman — not because she was never hurt, but because she chose to rise anyway.

The most important love you will ever know is the love you offer yourself. You deserve for that love to be gentle, unwavering, and true. So, let this be the beginning. Of healing. Of remembering. Of reclaiming your power. You are not starting over — you are becoming. And who you are becoming is breathtaking.

Remember: you are worthy. You are radiant. You are enough. You always have been. And you always will be.

With all my love,
Xoxo,
Ann-Kathrin

Story of Ellavate:

My story of elevating began in Australia, when I was in a women's shelter, running away from "home" with my three-month-old daughter. I sat on the bed with nothing but a bottle of water, some bread, fruit, and fresh nappies bought with a grocery voucher. I was shaking with fear, stunned that I had just left someone I once thought was my life partner. I was in shock, yet I felt safe for the first time in a very long while. That was when I asked myself: How did I get here? How did I end up with no friends, no family, no support, far away from my home country of Germany, fighting and defending myself and my baby?

A few hours earlier, I had been in a witness protection room — calm for the first time in years. The room was full of other women speaking to lawyers, police officers, and social workers. Children, from newborns to nine years old, were in the middle of it all. Some women cried; others tried to hold it together, repeating, "It's fine. No, I don't want to talk. I just want him to stop."

Despite the sadness, I felt secure. My heart rate, my stomach ache, and my nervousness eased slightly. Even though I told myself, "I don't belong here," I had to face the reality: this was exactly where I was. It was the first glimpse of change. I could no longer pretend everything was okay. That was when the first nudge came. I began asking a different question: How did I get here? What part did I play in ending up here? Where did it all go wrong on my end?

This was the shift.

Instead of asking, "Why does HE not stop behaving this way? Why does HE not act like a decent human being? What is wrong with HIM?" I began to look at myself. I realised what I had to do. That was when help became available, when I could finally accept support. I learnt about abuse in relationships, about codependency, about my patterns (it wasn't the first time I had been in a police station seeking protection). I learnt about childhood trauma, about "doing the inner work." I discovered that, while I was a victim of domestic violence, I was not a victim of life. I could change.

Over the next few years, I got out of abusive relationships, broke the toxic cycle, worked through PTSD, and began healing my codependency. I left the dating drama behind. I was also able to recognise these patterns in other women (and men) around me — and guide them through the same journey.

That is why I founded **ELLAVATE**: to create a supportive community for women who want to rise, especially those determined to break the cycle of trauma and not pass it on to the next generation.

My wish for my daughter, Ella, is that she grows up safe, stable, and surrounded by love, with a happy, grounded mother to look up to. I want to be her safe haven. But I knew I could not be that mother if I stayed stuck in abuse. I also knew the cycle would repeat if I didn't change. If I didn't stop the trauma here and now, I feared she might face the same — or worse.

I chose to elevate for the love of my life, my daughter Ella.

I believe that when we become mothers, we change in ways unimaginable beforehand. Within our growing community, we lovingly joke about creating names for our movement — "Johnevate" for a mum whose son is John, or "Emmavate" for a mum whose daughter is Emma. You get the point.

Let me tell you, **I ELLAVATED**.

And I continue to do so. My mission is to take many more women and mums on this journey, so our children can be freed from generational trauma — raised by stable, present parents who are no longer trapped by their past but lead the next generation with awareness and love.

I saw how many women (and men) are desperate to break free from dating drama and relationship misery. I saw how children are being impacted, and how cycles will keep spinning if we don't act. That is why I joined a group of women ready to take life into their own hands, to break free, and finally tap into our full potential.

That's what Team Ellavate is all about.

Welcome To Team Ellavate, Babe!

Thank you for choosing this journey and helping make the world better — by showing up with self-love, wholeness, and the courage to let go of what no longer serves you.

Your ripple effect touches everyone around you. You radiate differently, and your impact may be greater than you even realise. So thank you for stepping up and elevating — you do this for all of us, even if you don't yet see it yourself.

This book is for you — the woman reclaiming her life after toxic love. You are not too broken to begin again. You are not too lost to find your way. This is where you rise.

I am so proud of you, wherever you are on this journey.

- If you are heartbroken over the man you thought was forever, I see you. The pain is real — but so is your strength.

- If you are afraid to start over, in love or in life, know this: you are worthy of more.

- If you have escaped abuse and are sitting in a shelter, a friend's home, or even your car, lost and uncertain — this is not the end, this is your beginning.

- If you are in a hotel room with nothing but a suitcase, or crying on the floor of an empty new home, I know how heavy this moment feels. Let it be heavy for a while, knowing the light will return.

- If you are in a courthouse, terrified but still taking steps to protect yourself, you are stronger than you know.

- If you are still in the relationship, reading this with the sinking feeling that this is your story, listen to that voice. You are not mad — and you do not have to stay.

- If you are reading this in secret, know this: you are not alone. When you are ready, there will be a way out.

I have been through these phases. When I speak and write about them, it is because I lived through them — and elevated after them. If I can do it, so can you. You can turn all of this around, starting today. Believe in help, and it will appear in the most unexpected and magical ways. Let support come to you now.

In this phase, surround yourself with safe people. Or, if needed, give yourself permission to step back and tend to your wounded heart.

"The wound is the place where the Light enters you." — Rumi.

It may sound familiar, but there is truth in it: let your wound make you stronger. In Japan, the art of *Kintsugi* repairs broken pottery with gold, making it more beautiful for having been broken.

Tend to your wound with gold — and carry it with pride.

No matter how hard it feels, remember this: you've got this. By reading this book, you've already taken the first step towards healing. There is support, there is a better way, and you are not behind — you are only beginning.

You can ELLAVATE. And you don't have to do it alone. I am proud of you, and I love you.

Let's ELLAVATE!

In Pursuit of You:

Morning Mantra: *"I break free. I heal. I rise. I reclaim my worth. I own my life."*

Say it again. And again. Until you believe it. Until it becomes your truth.

This next chapter is called *In Pursuit of You* because that is what this journey is about. The chaos, heartbreak, and repeating patterns are not random — they are symptoms of something deeper.

If love has felt like struggle, confusion, or pain, it is not bad luck or bad partners. It is a sign that something within you is asking to be seen and healed. What you are truly searching for is not just romance. You are seeking a home — a place where you feel accepted, safe, understood, and cherished. Where love brings peace, not survival mode.

I do not mean a physical home. I mean a home within yourself. Some call this confidence, self-love, self-respect, or simply the deep knowing that you are enough.

For years, I thought I was searching for "the One," but really, I was searching for the parts of myself I had given away. I silenced my voice. Abandoned my needs. Shrunk myself just to be loved.

Maybe you have done that too. That is why this time is different. Because now, it is about you.

All the buzzwords — attachment styles, codependency, narcissism — can help, but knowledge alone is not enough. The real transformation begins when you ask:

How do I feel whole again?
How do I build a life I love, with or without a relationship?

This is your wake-up call. The time to stop outsourcing love. To stop waiting for someone else to give you what only you can give yourself.

It is time to pour all the energy you gave to others back into yourself. To stop chasing approval, to stop begging to be chosen, and to choose yourself — fully and unapologetically.

Maybe you have tried to outrun the emptiness. Chasing love. Keeping busy. Pleasing everyone. Working non-stop. Partying. But none of it filled the void — because what you were missing was you. The pain was not pointless. It was never your fault, but it was trying to tell you something. This is your chance to listen before life has to scream again.

I have been there too. From toxic love to rock bottom, I understand. And the turning point did not come from a new city, a new man, or a new job. It came when I stopped running and started looking within.

This phase is your mirror. Your reset. Your return. It is a reminder that the most important relationship you will ever have is the one with yourself.

So take this time. Date yourself. Know yourself. Fall in love with your own life. Because when you are whole, a romantic relationship becomes the bonus — not the lifeline.

Are you ready?

Let us begin.

Step 1 – Get Out of the (Shitty) Relationship:

Leaving unhealthy relationships — men who drained me, encounters that went nowhere — elevated my entire life.

I wish you could skip this step. I wish you were brand new to dating, starting fresh, untouched by heartache. I wish you never had to learn the way I did.

But if you are reading this, I assume you have faced dating drama and relationship mess. Many of us have lived through heartbreak so deep it felt like it shattered us entirely.

Here is where I went wrong from the start: I never questioned what love truly was. I never learnt about healthy love, and I did not even realise there was such a thing as unhealthy love.

I believed love meant:

- Butterflies and emotional highs.
- Finding someone to make me happy, to "complete" me.
- Staying, no matter the red flags, because "love conquers all."
- Tolerating pain in the name of devotion, loyalty and love.
- Healing or saving my partner to prove my worth/ to prove my love.
- Sacrificing my needs, voice, and joy.
- Giving endlessly, even when it wasn't returned.
- Chasing attention and affection.
- Feeling responsible for someone else's emotions.
- Suppressing myself to avoid conflict.

- Waiting to be "saved" by a partner.
- Thinking emotional chaos = passion.
- Putting them first—even when it hurt me.
- Confusing anxiety with excitement.
- Thinking, "If I just try harder, they'll love me right"
- Losing myself in the name of love

But *rea aka healthy* love is:

- Safe, grounded, emotionally secure.
- A beautiful addition to a life you already love.
- Mutual effort and daily choice.
- Rooted in honesty, respect, and trust.
- Boundaries that protect, not distance.
- Growing together, without losing yourself.
- Peace, not turmoil.
- Being accepted for who you are.
- Communicating without fear.
- Stability—not an exhausting push and pull.
- Feeling supported, not drained.
- Knowing disagreements don't have to turn into war.
- A true partnership—us vs. the problem, not me vs. you.
- Alignment of words and actions.
- Equal effort—no more one-sided love.
- A love that expands your life, not consumes it.
- Freedom, not entrapment.
- A love that adds to your joy, not one you suffer through.

Healthy love doesn't require you to lose yourself. It helps you find yourself while being loved by someone who supports and honours who you are — exactly as you are, right now.

I was naïve. I didn't know love could be dangerous. I didn't realise my idea of love was built on childhood wounds, limiting beliefs, old protective patterns, and the influence of societal norms and images. I never asked whether what I thought was "normal" love was actually healthy.

Maybe you are starting to ask those questions now. If so, I am proud of you. I hope this chapter helps you see love — and yourself — differently.

If you are fortunate enough never to have experienced abuse, may this keep you safe. If you are in a relationship that feels off, may this bring you clarity. And if you are in an abusive relationship, may this be the lifeline that helps you out.

I am going to talk about abuse and violence in this chapter — physical, emotional, and psychological. If that feels too heavy, come back when you are ready. You can skip ahead and learn about EFT Tapping (Emotional Freedom Technique), a tool I will introduce later to calm your nervous system when triggered.

This chapter is here to help you recognise unhealthy patterns. Maybe you have been in toxic cycles. Maybe you have stayed too long in something that felt wrong. Maybe you are still hoping they will change. I understand. I have been through it too.

This clarity is not only for those caught in abuse, but also for those on the sidelines, watching a friend being pulled in without realising it.

If you have never experienced this, I am not trying to scare you — but you need to know it is real. The media sells us drama as passion.

We are told love is the cure for our wounds, but with the wrong person, love can become a prison.

In many countries, abuse, marital rape, coercion, and violence are still considered normal. Even in places where equality is more common, abuse remains a daily struggle. In Germany, a woman is killed every third day by an ex-partner. We are taught to endure, to stay, to fix — but not to leave. We are not taught how to choose wisely, or when to walk away. That is why I wrote this book.

If you have children, hear this especially: leaving isn't just for you, it is for them. They deserve to see you safe, loved, and whole. They deserve to know love doesn't come with bruises — on the body or on the spirit. Children exposed to domestic violence are more likely to become either victims or perpetrators later in life.

So let's be clear: when a relationship is abusive or toxic, there is only one answer — get out.

I will repeat this until you hear it in your bones. But let me be clear: I am not saying leave simply because it is hard. Relationships can be hard. Growth requires patience and vulnerability. I advise leaving when the relationship becomes dangerous, or when you are the only one fighting to keep it alive.

Here is the truth: it takes two. You cannot fix a relationship alone. I know this because I tried. I believed that if I just worked harder on myself — became more patient, more giving, more "perfect" — maybe it would heal. But love is not a one-person job. Abuse of any kind is not love.

If there is physical violence, emotional abuse, manipulation, gaslighting, or coercion — it is not something to fix, it is something to leave.

Healthy love is built on a solid foundation — your foundation. Most people get this wrong. They try to build forever on shaky ground, putting up the rooftop terrace before laying the base. It looks fine for a while, but when the storm comes, it crumbles.

Ask yourself honestly: are you standing on solid ground, or teetering on a plank, hoping it doesn't break?

I spent years searching for "the One," believing I needed a partner to be whole. I thought I could only build my life if someone else helped me. That belief led me into situationships that dragged on, partners who drained me, or worse, harmed me.

I thought love meant endurance — proving myself through sacrifice. It left me waiting to start my life, giving up my power, my time, and bouncing between lives that were never mine. No wonder it never worked. No wonder I was unhappy. And no wonder my partners were too.

When I hit rock bottom, I stopped making excuses. I stopped clinging to false hope. I tore down the unstable house I had built and laid a new foundation. I rebuilt myself first. Only then — only when I was solid — did I invite love in again.

Are you ready to do the same?

The Two Relationships You Must Walk Away From:

There are two kinds of relationships I strongly encourage you to walk away from:

1. **Toxic Relationships:** Where you feel disrespected, unseen, emotionally drained, or constantly on edge. Even without physical harm, emotional toxicity can be just as damaging. Many abusive relationships begin with subtle toxic traits that gradually intensify over time.

    a. **Abusive Relationships:** Abuse can take many forms — financial, emotional, physical, or sexual. It rarely begins with physical violence. More often, it starts with subtle control, manipulation, or emotional harm. It can involve humiliation, isolation, threats, intimidation, or shame — and over time, may escalate into domestic violence.

2. **Mediocre Relationships:** The ones you stay in not because you're happy, but because you're afraid of being alone.

All of the above cost you dearly. Your time. Your energy. Your self-worth. You weren't born to survive—you were born to *thrive*. You can't thrive in a toxic or abusive environment. If you are stuck in boring cycles repeating patterns of boring nonsense, it's hard to remember that you are meant to thrive.

Toxic vs. Abusive Relationships:

Toxic and abusive relationships live on the same spectrum, but there's a key distinction:

- **Toxicity** stems from unhealthy patterns—poor communication, disrespect, emotional volatility, or lack of boundaries.

- **Abuse** is about *control*. One person dominates the other through manipulation, gaslighting, threats, violence, or fear.

If your partner disrespects your boundaries, minimises your feelings, isolates you from loved ones, or makes you feel unsafe, that is abuse. Abuse is not just physical. Emotional wounds run deep.

I used to tell myself, "He doesn't hit me, so it's not abuse." That was my excuse. But the truth is, abuse can destroy your spirit long before it bruises your body.

Twice, in different countries and with different men, a judge had to tell me that being called names, threatened, and bullied was abuse too. Abuse does not only come in the form of physical violence. I was wrong in thinking otherwise, but I had to experience several forms of it — and hear it from police and judges — before I could accept the reality: I am an abused woman.

I remember sitting on my friend's couch when she told me again and again, "You are an abused woman. You need to stop making excuses for him and start living your life." Even then, I did not want to face it.

When I later worked in women's shelters, I learnt that it often takes women seven tries to actually leave an abusive relationship. It is "normal" to go back over and over. It takes a moment to realise you are being abused — and an incredible amount of courage, strength, and support to finally leave.

If you are crying yourself to sleep, constantly questioning your worth, or making excuses for someone's behaviour, it is time to stop searching for reasons to stay.

Stop Searching for Excuses—Start Searching for Your Power:

I spent years obsessing over definitions. *"Is he a narcissist?" "Maybe he just has trauma and needs more compassion to change?"* None of those labels changed how I felt: like shit.

If you are in that spiral, ask yourself: *Why am I justifying a relationship that makes me miserable? Why am I tolerating behaviour that harms me?*

You are not responsible for healing someone else's wounds. You are not a rehab centre for broken men. The only person you are responsible for is *you*.

Breaking the Cycle:

If you grew up with dysfunction, toxic love might feel familiar — even normal. But familiar does not mean safe.

Staying teaches your children, and yourself, that this is what love looks like. Unless someone breaks the cycle, it continues.

I know leaving can feel impossible. But as we have already established, staying in a toxic relationship is not an option — not if you want peace, not if you want freedom.

You are not stuck. You are not alone. There is a way out. One concept that helped me was understanding the **Cycle of Abuse**.

The Cycle of Abuse:

You can explore it here:

☞ [Cycle of Abuse – Making Wellness](#)

Abuse isn't random—it follows a predictable pattern. Understanding it can be your first step toward freedom. Here is how the cycle works:

1. **Tension Building:** The atmosphere shifts. The abuser becomes irritable, controlling, and distant. You feel like you are "walking on eggshells."

2. **Incident (Explosion):** Abuse occurs. It could be physical, verbal, emotional, sexual, or financial. The harm is real.

3. **Reconciliation (Honeymoon Phase):** The abuser apologizes, makes promises, or blames stress, drinking, or *you*. Gifts, tears, and declarations of love may follow. This phase creates false hope.

4. **Calm (False Peace):** Things seem fine again... for a while until the cycle resets. And know this: The cycle ALWAYS resets in this dynamic.

Each time the cycle repeats, the incident becomes more intense. More dangerous. More harmful. More painful.

You are not imagining this. You are not responsible for someone else's harmful behaviour.

This cycle will continue until someone stops it. And recognising it could save your life.

So how about you become that someone — and leave?

How to Break the Cycle:

- **Recognize the pattern**: Awareness is the beginning of change. Remember how many judges and police interventions I needed in order to recognize the pattern?
- **Seek support**: Therapists, support groups, trusted friends, Police, lawyers—don't go through it alone!
- **Set and protect your boundaries**: You need to voice your needs and establish your "no!"
- **Make a safety plan**: If you are in danger, prepare a way out and ask for professional help
- **Believe in yourself**: A life beyond abuse *is* possible. You deserve peace and healthy love!

Breaking the cycle is hard, but you are stronger than you think. Your story doesn't end here—it's only just beginning.

If Someone You Love Is in an Abusive Relationship:

Instead of asking, *"Why doesn't she leave?"* or *"What is wrong with her?"* — support her. Offer shelter, emotional support, and resources, like this book. Believe her. Remind her she deserves more. Understand that she is not an idiot. There is so much going on in her world that she doesn't speak about, and often she has no idea what is really happening.

One of the most common and misunderstood questions women in abusive relationships face is: *"Why doesn't she just leave?"* The truth is, leaving is not simply a choice — it can be the most dangerous moment of all. Statistically, the risk of being seriously harmed or even killed by an abusive partner is highest at the point of breaking up or shortly after. Abusers often escalate control when they feel it slipping. Escaping is a calculated risk, not a simple step. Add trauma bonding, fear, financial dependence, and eroded self-worth, and it's clear: she isn't weak — she's surviving.

"I don't think people have any idea how much strength it takes to survive in an abusive relationship. If you're trapped in one, please know you are not weak. I know you feel that way, but you're not. You're doing what's necessary to stay alive. Don't give up on getting out."
— *Sheleana Aiyana, Rising Woman*

A person in an abusive relationship is often not living but surviving. Their nervous system is stuck in overdrive — constantly on high alert, flooded with cortisol and adrenaline. This makes it difficult to think clearly, make healthy decisions, or be emotionally present.

From the outside, they may appear strong or put together, but inside they are carrying an invisible weight. Most don't even realise they are operating from survival mode because it has become their normal. They are not being distant or difficult on purpose — they are battling internal chaos you cannot see. Simply existing in that state takes their full capacity.

This is why instead of adding pressure, we must offer compassion. Unhealthy relationships keep people trapped in survival, unable to look beyond the chaos. Do not expect emotional availability, deep connection, or compassion from someone still in abuse. What you can do is understand, not add more demands, and gently support.

A powerful metaphor that explains why people stay is the "frog method." If you put a frog in boiling water, it jumps out. But if you place it in lukewarm water and slowly raise the heat, it stays — unaware it's being boiled alive. Abuse works the same way. It rarely begins with shouting or hitting. It starts with subtle control, manipulation, gaslighting, and withdrawal. Slowly, the person adapts, rationalises, and becomes desensitised. By the time the abuse is obvious, they are already entangled, drained of self-trust, and unsure how to leave.

To the woman reading this who feels trapped: your safety is the priority. You do not have to do this alone. Reach out. Call someone you trust. Involve the police if you feel unsafe. Contact a women's shelter or an organisation that can help you plan your exit.

When I left, I once asked the police if I could return just to grab a few things. Their response stopped me cold: *"No. Your safety comes first. We'll go with you later. Or you leave the things behind. Your life is more important than your belongings."* I broke down, but something shifted. For the first time, I realised I was in danger — and that I was worth protecting. So are you.

Your freedom is possible. You don't have to earn it alone. Build a circle around you. Let people help you.

If children are involved, there is an added responsibility — both for you and the person in the dynamic. But whether or not children are present, here is the focus: what you can do.

- Be transparent about what you think about the situation.

- When she is ready to leave, offer her shelter or help her find one.

- Encourage her to listen to her intuition.

- Don't judge her.

Ask questions:

- If your daughter or best friend were in your exact situation, what would you want for her?

- What would you say to a woman who told you her partner treats her the way yours does?

- If you knew you would be ok – physically, emotionally, mentally, and financially – would you still choose to stay?

- What kind of love do you want your children to learn is normal?

- What part of you believes that this is the best you can get?

It is not your job to save her. It is not your job to become her therapist or force her to see what she is not ready to see.

It took me decades to finally recognise my patterns and change them. Many people offered me resources, which I ignored again and again. Once I was ready, I knew whom I could ask for support.

What helped were the simple words: *"I see what is going on. I know what is happening. If you ever want out, let me know. I love you. We are here for you."* Those words became my lifeline when I finally had to leave.

This is all you need to do for now: be there for her. If she is ready to leave, help calmly. Know where a shelter is. Understand that she is in survival mode and may need gentle guidance more than anything else.

Always remember: she can only save herself. She has an intuition she has forgotten to trust. Encouraging her to listen to that inner voice, to her gut feeling, is the best gift you can give.

My Story—and the Scars That Still Speak:

Like many survivors of domestic violence, I didn't see the danger right away. I thought it was just one bad night, one incident (and after all, I did provoke him, right?). I thought it would get better. Even now, years later, I still hear their voices in my head:

> "You're overreacting."
> "No one will believe you."
> "It's your fault."
> "You made me do this."
> "If you tell anyone, it will just get worse!"

I have had to double-check my own memories — text messages, legal reports, friends' confirmations — just to validate what really happened. That's how deep the gaslighting went. Even now, I fear speaking out. I wonder if my abusers will come for me again. I hear the whispers, feel the shame, and battle the doubt.

There were many times during the writing of this book when I told myself I would never publish it. I thought silence would protect me — that if I never spoke about it, I would never be punished or contacted by my abusers again.

But then I remembered: the trauma still lives in my body. What I went through was real. Many other women are going through it too, and I need to speak up.

A big part of the trauma was being silenced. I believed no one would be there for me. I feared that speaking up would only make things worse.

But now I know: I have to speak — for myself and for other women. Speaking up is safe. Speaking up is necessary. Speaking up is part of breaking the cycle.

Other women need to hear there is a way out, just like I once needed to hear it too.

Understanding the Love-Bombing Phase and Letting Go:

It didn't start out as abuse. He was funny, sweet, and attentive. He made me feel alive — and that is what makes it so hard to leave.

We crave the beginning — the "honeymoon," the movie-magic moments. We experienced what felt like love, which made it harder to let go. We kept hoping those happy moments would return.

We blamed ourselves, wondering if we had triggered the shift. We made excuses, longing for things to go back to the way they were. But that version of him was a mask.

Maybe I was emotionally overwhelmed and missed the red flags hidden between moments of affection. The kindness, the laughter — they were part of the pattern. That is what hooked you.

Whether conscious or not, the cycle of abuse always begins with this love-bombing stage.

Realizing this shifted my perspective:

After my final abusive relationship — where domestic violence was the reason I left — I finally let go of my illusions. I no longer just understood the cycle in my mind; this time, I felt it. I had lived it too many times.

When that truth landed, I stopped justifying his behaviour. I stopped blaming myself. I stopped hoping he would change. I said, *"No more."*

No more men letting their pain destroy my peace.
No more tiptoeing around someone else's rage.
No more numbing myself with alcohol or substances.
No more sacrificing my dignity for a sliver of affection.

I lost trust. I lost respect. I lost the safety that I now believe is non-negotiable in love. But I also gained something: myself.

This was a turning point — the moment I let go of toxic patterns, stepped away from relationship chaos, and finally broke free from the cycle of abuse.

Most Abusers Use These Stages:

My story, like that of so many others, shows that abuse doesn't always begin with a slap or a scream. More often, it arrives disguised as love.

It creeps in slowly. What begins as a small red flag or a subtle incident grows over time — especially once emotional, financial, mental, and physical entanglement has taken hold.

Here are some of the common stages and tactics abusers use to manipulate, isolate, and control:

1. Charming The Victim In (Aka Love Bombing):

At first, they seem perfect. Incredibly charming. Attentive. Thoughtful. They see you as no one ever has. You are celebrated for who you are, showered with affection, gifts, and compliments.

This is called *love bombing* — the abuser's opening act. It's intoxicating. You feel special, chosen, finally seen.

But this phase is not love — it is control, disguised as romance.

2. Isolating the Victim:

Next comes the slow unravelling of your connections to the outside world. You might move to another city, state, or even another country. It feels like a fresh start, but in reality, it separates you from your friends, family, work, and community.

It is never framed as control. It sounds like:

"Let's build a life together."
"This new job is an amazing opportunity for me."
"I just want to protect you."

Soon, you are far from anyone who might witness the bruises — or hear the screams. Isolation is strategic.

Sometimes it is dramatic, like living off-grid. Other times it is more subtle:

"Your family is toxic."
"Your friends don't support us."
"You've outgrown them."

After the love bombing, it can feel flattering that they "still love you despite all your flaws." But this is where the trap tightens.

3. Creating Dependence:

Financial, emotional, or parental dependence is a major reason women stay in abusive relationships.

- You move into his home.
- You share a business.

- You become a stay-at-home mom.
- You quit your job to "focus on love" or "on the family."

Suddenly, leaving feels impossible. You hear yourself say, *"If it weren't for the kids..."* or *"If I had money, I'd go."*

That is exactly what they want: your dependence.

4. **Rules Disguised as "Help":**

These start small, disguised as concern:

- Don't wear that—it makes you look stupid.

- Your family holds you back. You're better off without them.

- Don't go to the gym—men will hit on you and that makes me feel uncomfortable.

- Let me help you be more confident—start with losing the glasses.

They say it is out of love, but it is about control. Bit by bit, your autonomy is stripped away.

What is really happening? They are eroding your identity, crushing your confidence, and creating a reality where they become your only trusted voice.

5. **The Emotional Roller Coaster (Back to Love Bombing):**

When the abuse starts creeping in — verbal attacks, disrespect, jealousy — you think about leaving.

Then suddenly, they are sweet again:

"I'm sorry."
"I didn't mean it."
"You make me crazy — but I love you so much."

This hot-and-cold cycle creates confusion and addiction. You begin to crave the highs just to survive the lows. Your brain rewires itself to chase approval, begging for crumbs from the man who once adored you.

It becomes a chemical rollercoaster — dopamine, adrenaline, cortisol — all tangled in your heart. And it keeps you hooked.

6. Gaslighting:

Gaslighting is psychological warfare. The goal? To make you doubt yourself so completely that you begin to believe their version of reality.

Here is how it shows up:

- **Denial:** *"That never happened. You're imagining things."*
- **Minimisation:** *"You're overreacting."*
- **Deflection:** *"You're just insecure."*
- **Rewriting history:** *"I never said that. You must be confused."*

Sound familiar? Ever been called "crazy"? Gaslighting makes you question everything—your memory, your instincts, your worth.

7. Breadcrumbing:

Breadcrumbing is when someone gives you just enough attention, affection, or communication to keep you interested. It's like being tossed "breadcrumbs" instead of the full meal.

This tactic is manipulative. The abuser gives just enough to keep you around without ever committing or showing up consistently. The moment you decide to leave, they do something to remind you of how great they *can* be. They show just enough love to keep you hooked.

When you start pulling back, they suddenly pour on the attention. But as soon as you show interest again, they withdraw — and the effort drops.

You will know you are being breadcrumbed if:

- They text randomly at 10 p.m. after long silences

- They make promises but avoid making concrete plans "Let's plan a trip one day" but it never happens.

- They're warm and caring one day, cold the next. When

- The connection leaves you confused, and you wonder where you stand with them

- They are vague about their intentions or a future with you

- The conversations are playful and fun but they stay at surface level. No deeper emotional connection is built

They want validation, attention, control, and emotional power — without offering anything real. Over time, this creates emotional whiplash, erodes self-esteem, and keeps you stuck hoping for more than they will ever give.

When you finish this book, you will no longer chase these games. If you want commitment and he offers crumbs — it's a no.

8. Disconnection from Your Self & Life:

The more disconnected you are from your identity, your friends, and your goals, the better it works for them. They do not want a powerful woman.

They want you broken, doubtful, small. Abused women are not weak. In fact, it often thrills abusers to bring strong, successful women to their knees. It is a challenge. It makes them feel powerful.

These are only some of the tactics abusers use. You may already have had your *AHA* moment. You may see your current relationship in these pages. You may even recognise your own behaviours. If so, there is no shame in that.

The most intelligent, capable, successful women have been victims of abuse. Abuse is not about intelligence — it is about manipulation, emotional entanglement, and a society that romanticises drama as passion.

It is time to take the shame off survivors and to educate ourselves, our friends, our daughters. Because the home — a place meant to be your sanctuary — should never become a prison.

Kids and Abuse:

When children are involved, the stakes are even higher. It becomes our responsibility — not just as partners, but as parents — to create a safe space.

An abusive household isn't just hard on you. It builds anxiety, sadness, fear, and trauma in your children. Even if you think you are protecting them, they feel it. They know.

One of the most heartbreaking reasons I hear for staying in abusive relationships is this:

"*I'm staying for the kids.*"

Let's be brutally honest: you are not helping your children by staying. You are hurting them. When your children witness you being disrespected, yelled at, belittled, manipulated, or harmed, they internalise that as normal.

You are teaching them what love looks like. You are showing them what a woman "should" tolerate. You are shaping their future relationships. You are keeping the trauma train moving.

Even if you think they don't see it, they do.

"He's not mean to the kids."
"They don't know he's using drugs."
"They don't see how he treats me."

Baby — they know. Children are not stupid. They are intuitive. They may not understand every word, but they feel the energy. They hear the tension. They absorb the chaos.

Leaving Isn't Just for You. It's for Them:

Your children deserve to see you happy, safe, strong, and loved. Whether you are partnered or alone does not matter. What matters is that they witness you choosing peace over pain, confidence over fear, and self-worth over survival.

Staying in a toxic relationship doesn't protect them — it programs them.

- It teaches that suffering in love is normal.
- That silence is strength.
- That love hurts.
- That fear is part of the family.

From the womb to age seven, a child's subconscious is being formed. These are their imprint years — the time when the blueprint of what love looks like, feels like, and sounds like is written.

If what they witness is control, shouting, dishonesty, manipulation — or even violence — they will accept that as truth. They may repeat the pattern in adulthood, or go numb to it altogether.

You Are Their Safe Place:

As mothers, we carry a sacred responsibility — not just to ourselves, but to the next generation. Your children cannot leave, but you can. They cannot save themselves. That is your job.

You were given their trust. Their love. Their safety. If the world is unfair, unpredictable, or unsafe, then home cannot be. If your home does not feel safe, calm, or secure, you must change that — for them and for you.

This is what I had to do. Before I could heal, rebuild, or become the woman I am today, I got out. That was the very first step.

This is your reminder: if you have children, leaving a toxic or abusive home is no longer just a choice. It is a necessity. Because when you save yourself, you save them too.

Things I Did While Being in Toxic Relationships:

If you have experienced abuse or become entangled in toxic — even dangerous — relationships, these may be patterns you have followed, or still follow, in your relationships.

- **Googled Their Behavior**:

I spent countless nights searching: *Is what he did okay? What does this mean? Why does someone behave like this? Is this gaslighting? What is emotional abuse? Why does he breadcrumb me?*

I was too ashamed to open up to friends — or even to him — so I turned to Google instead of having real conversations.

- **Hid My Feelings and Opinions:**

I became an expert at emotional suppression. I walked around as if carrying a bomb, hoping nothing and no one would set it off.

I constantly walked on eggshells, unable to speak my truth. I stayed silent during outbursts — some directed at me, others not. Even when it wasn't physical, the emotional instability made me feel deeply unsafe.

Sometimes it was physical — objects thrown, walls punched, threats made. In those moments, I didn't advocate for myself. I adapted. I minimised. I fixed. I stayed. And each time I did, I lost a piece of myself.

When I faced issues, challenges, or had things on my mind, I didn't talk about them or express what I truly needed. In the beginning, I tried — but my words were ignored or met with anger.

Instead of walking away, I convinced myself to stay. I pushed aside my own feelings and needs, just as they did. Shutting up, silencing myself, became my normal.

- **Being an Emotional Wreck:**

I cried often. I felt mistreated, misunderstood, and completely alone. Overwhelmed and emotionally scattered.

I was afraid to speak about what I needed, so I shut down — yet still showed intense emotions. Over time, I built up deep resentment towards the person I was with.

Anxiety and depressive moods became constant. I felt too unsafe to talk about my inner world.

- **Excused His Behavior:**

I crafted stories to protect my partners. I covered for their addictions, their emotional outbursts, and even their criminal behaviour.

I understood them — too much. I knew their trauma, their childhood wounds. I wanted to heal the pain and help them.

I knew they had done wrong, but I still covered it up. I believed that made me loyal.

- **Stayed in my Codependent Behavior:**

What I did was everything a codependent person does. When I finally left my last toxic relationship, I had a brutal realisation: I was addicted to being the fixer.

I helped them rebuild their lives while neglecting my own. I put my dreams, my friendships, and my well-being on hold. I enabled addiction. I became a one-woman rescue mission, convincing myself that was love.

To my surprise, it wasn't.

There is an entire chapter on codependency ahead — but this, right here, is how it showed up in my life.

Trauma Bonding:

Trauma bonding is that invisible thread that ties you to someone who hurts you. It is not love — it is a psychological trap. An addictive loop of pain and pleasure.

One day, they are kind. They remind you of how things used to be. You feel special. Next, they withdraw, lash out, or disappear entirely. This cycle of highs and lows creates a powerful emotional grip. It is the *hope* of returning to the good times that keeps you stuck.

Trauma bonding can look like real connection, but it is rooted in unresolved emotional pain. It creates an intense exchange — through texting, presence, and constant interaction — that activates the brain's reward system.

Each ping on your phone, each touch, and each *"I love you"* delivers a small dopamine hit, like pulling a slot machine. This builds anticipation and gratification loops that may feel like closeness, but are more about stimulation than true intimacy.

If the texting or connection feels addictive, overwhelming, or emotionally draining, it may be trauma bonding.

Remember the love-bombing phase? That emotional high is often the result of trauma bonding, not genuine love.

If you have thought:

- *"But they weren't always like this..."*

- *"If I love them enough, maybe they'll change."*

- *"They just need time. They're struggling."*

- *"I feel so connected to them — I can't leave now."*

...you may be caught in a trauma bond. Trauma bonds create confusion, self-doubt, and a dangerous dependency. You crave the crumbs of affection because they once felt like a feast.

Breaking free feels like withdrawal — because it is. Your brain has been rewired.

But the way out is through: cut the tie, create space, and remind yourself that real love does not feel like survival.

Involving the Police?

I get it. It is terrifying. The doubts begin to swirl:

- *Will this make things worse?*
- *Will I even be believed?*
- *Am I blowing things out of proportion?*
- *If I leave, does that mean the relationship is really over?*

I have asked all of these questions. I have been there. Still, involving the police saved my life.

I delayed calling them. I excused theft, threats, and violence. But once I reported it, I felt safe for the first time in years. My assets were protected. I finally realised that what I was experiencing was abuse. Involving the police gave me clarity, protection, and empowerment. Twice, it changed my life.

If you are scared — if you are being threatened, financially controlled, or physically harmed — get support. Call. Go to a shelter. Tell someone. It is not weakness, it is strength.

Once, I dated a man who those around me knew was no good; involved in scams, drugs, and other illegal activities. Before saying anything to me, my family and close friends tried to confirm the rumours were true. They even conducted a background check on him — but found nothing.

What happened instead was that I ended up in the police station, with money and assets stolen from me, trapped in another abusive relationship. I could have been warned, had there been actual facts available.

Involving the police is not only about your protection — it also creates a record. A record of someone who is out to harm people, and who will continue to do so once you are gone.

Had the women who experienced the same things with my ex filed police reports, they might have saved me — and those who came after me.

Since then, I have believed it is not only self-protection, but also an obligation to others, to report.

Know Your Rights:

You have rights. But you must know them, seek them out, and use them.

In toxic or abusive relationships, it is common to feel powerless. But the truth is, the law is on your side. In countries such as Germany, the United States, Canada, and much of Europe, you have legal protection from emotional, physical, sexual, and financial abuse.

You can call the police, apply for a restraining order, seek emergency housing, and protect your children. These rights are not just words on paper — they are tools for your freedom.

I did not know about my rights. I did not use them. I was too ashamed, sometimes afraid. Most of the time, I stayed silent because I felt stupid for having let it happen.

Elevating means not only reclaiming your voice, but also making use of the protection that already exists. You are not alone. You are not crazy. You are not powerless.

Know your rights — and do not let fear or shame stop you from using them.

When the Relationship Isn't Dangerous—Just *Meh:*

Not all relationships are toxic. Not every relationship ends in abuse. Some are simply... mediocre. You are not in danger, but you are not growing either.

There is no excitement. No shared vision. You are not fulfilled — you are simply not alone. That becomes the justification.

If you have experienced abuse before, a relationship that feels "safe but unsatisfying" can seem like a relief.

But I want to remind you of something important: you are meant for more.

As my best friend once said to me, *"There is more out there for you,"* when I was settling into a relationship with a man who felt safe but was also incredibly boring.

You didn't pick up this book to learn how to settle. You picked it up to elevate.

Ask yourself:

- *How does he contribute to my well-being?*
- *What do I genuinely like about him?*
- *Does he meet my standards?* (We will explore this in more depth later in the book.)
- *Am I "future-tripping"?* (Dreaming about a potential future that was never actually discussed?)
- *Do I enjoy being with him when sex is not involved?*
- *Do I truly enjoy being intimate with him?*
- *Am I outsourcing my happiness?* (Do I make him responsible for it?)
- *Can I grow and thrive while staying in this relationship?*

- *Do I shine — or shrink — when he is around?*
- *Are we working towards the same life goals?*
- *Does this relationship expand me, or drain me?*
- *How do I feel when he is not around?* (Am I at peace, or constantly worrying about him or us?)
- *Does he put me on a pedestal?*
- *Is he losing himself by being with me?*

The 10/90 Rule:

Here is a concept that changed everything for me: **10% for them, 90% for you.**

That means:

- *No more talking about your ex in every conversation.*
- *No more over-analysing what happened.*
- *No more giving your past the spotlight.*
- *No more dissecting why your ex did what they did.*

We've all been there — or known someone who couldn't stop talking about their ex after a breakup. Processing what happened is important, even necessary. But there comes a point when the story has to pause so that healing can begin.

Give it 10%. Let yourself feel. Journal. Cry. Talk in therapy. But then, return to *you*. Because that is where the real healing begins.

Eventually, that 10% drops to zero. And when it does? You are free.

No more spiralling. No more self-blame. No more being stuck in their shadow. You did it. You got out.

You have completed Step One. Now… let's step into the life that is waiting for you.

Step 2 – Dating Sabbatical:

A Dating Sabbatical is a conscious, intentional break from all romantic and sexual entanglements. It is the decision to step away from dating, drama, and distractions — and turn all that attention inward.

Think of it as emotional rehab: no dating apps, no "accidental" flings, no scrolling through your ex's Instagram, and definitely no seeking validation from another person.

This is a man-free time. This is the season to focus on yourself — to rebuild from the inside out.

Why Take a Dating Sabbatical?

You are not pausing love — you are reclaiming your power and building a solid foundation, so love can eventually feel safe. It's been messy so far, hasn't it? Which is why it is time to do something different.

The Dating Sabbatical is a sacred time to heal, to reflect, and to lay a foundation before entering any future relationship. You wouldn't build a house without solid ground — why build a relationship without stability within?

You will feel the pull, especially during holidays, family gatherings, or warm summer nights. Valentine's Day. Christmas. Spring flings.

The pressure to "have someone" will creep in. Add societal expectations like, *"Why are you still single?"* — and it's easy to fall back into old patterns. But this time, you choose differently.

Many of us date to distract. We swipe for dopamine. We chase hook-ups, attention, and flirtation to avoid sitting in our discomfort. A Dating Sabbatical invites you to face those feelings head-on. It requires honesty. Courage. A willingness to do what most people avoid. It isn't just a break — it's an emotional reset. The space you need to unhook from external validation and reconnect with your own voice.

During this time, I began to notice my patterns and the ways I was self-sabotaging in different parts of my life. I felt my emotions instead of avoiding them. I stopped distracting myself by chasing love, and I discovered what actually made me feel happy. It wasn't comfortable. Then again, growth never is.

As someone who prioritised my partners' happiness over my own (hello, codependency!), I had to face some difficult emotions and realisations. Previously, I couldn't stop dating; I went from one relationship to another, even after those that hurt me. Despite the chaos and pain, I clung to love like it was oxygen. People romanticised it: *"She hasn't given up on love."* But the truth? I was addicted. Love had become a drug. I needed a serious detox.

I couldn't build healthy love until I built a healthy me. If you find it difficult to take a break from men, dating, and relationships, there may be something deeper at play.

You might be struggling with love addiction — also known as codependency. I know the word *addiction* can feel scary, but acknowledging it is how you change it.

Look into support groups such as:

- **SLAA:** *Sex and Love Addicts Anonymous*
- **CODA:** *Codependents Anonymous*

Both also offer online meetings if attending in person isn't possible. Don't let shame or excuses hold you back. This is your healing season. You are here because you are ready to rise.

I've been through this myself, and I can tell you from experience: gaining awareness, releasing shame, and truly choosing to grow beyond these patterns can transform your life far beyond dating and relationships.

I changed my entire way of living once I stopped people-pleasing and acting from codependent habits. I highly recommend exploring topics like anxious attachment and codependency, which we'll dive into later in this book, to see if any of it resonates with you.

No More "Backups":

During this time, you don't keep numbers "just in case." You don't swipe when you are sad or bored. You don't call someone you don't truly want, just to feel wanted.

You are choosing solitude over survival mode and dopamine hits.

You are choosing to know yourself before trying to know someone else. You are choosing foundation before fantasy.

How to Handle Triggers and Emotions:

When you're used to getting a lot of attention while dating, in relationships, or from men in general, you may need to shift a few things. Even negative attention is still attention — it creates a dopamine hit, an adrenaline rush, or a sense of stimulation. You might notice uncomfortable emotions like loneliness or the fear of running out of time.

Your role during this phase is to feel what comes up — and to notice the thought patterns and beliefs that arise from those emotions.

When emotions become too overwhelming to handle, try this exercise: **let the feeling be.**

Instead of analysing it or pushing it away, allow it in. Imagine it as a wave coming towards you. I like to lie down or sit in a comfortable chair for this, making sure I feel safe and grounded. Picture the wave rolling in. Like the tide crashing on the shore, let it come and let it pass.

Sometimes it might feel like the wave is smashing into a rock. Other times, it may feel like it swallows you whole, spinning you around before releasing you. That's okay. Let the experience be whatever it is.

You might feel the urge to cry, move, scream, or hit a pillow. All of that is valid — often necessary. Let the emotions come.

Move your body if you need to. Dance if that helps. Once you let the feelings out, they stop building up inside you.

Another great way to handle emotional overwhelm is by using the tools we'll explore in the next chapter. My personal favourite is EFT Tapping, and I cannot recommend it enough.

Let's be real: this will be hard. The phrase, *"The best way to get over a guy is to get under a guy,"* is toxic nonsense. It only repeats the same story with a new face.

When I started my Dating Sabbatical, I was met with resistance. A part of me panicked:

"If I don't date now, I'll be alone forever."

Maybe you can relate? I journalled every fear. Every belief. Every excuse. I urge you to do the same. Write it down. Face it. You'll be shocked at what's living in your subconscious. Those stories? They aren't true. But we live as if they are — until we unlearn them.

When you feel the urge to text someone or get back on the apps, ask yourself:

- *Do I want to text someone just to feel validated?*
- *Do I open dating apps when I'm bored, lonely, or feeling rejected?*
- *What's behind this habit or urge?*
- *Do I eat, shop, scroll, take drugs, play games, or party to avoid being alone?*
- *Do I silence my needs just to feel connected?*
- *Do I freeze, fawn, or self-abandon when triggered?*

Watch yourself. Get curious, not critical. Observe how your body responds to discomfort. Journal. Breathe through it. Let the urge come — and resist acting on it.

This phase is about building emotional self-regulation. About learning to self-soothe without running into someone else's arms. Once you become aware of how and when you use the apps (or dating in general), you'll notice this self-awareness spilling into every other part of your life too.

The Ellavate Challenge:

During my Dating Sabbatical, I tried everything: coaching, therapy, somatic experiences, tapping, journalling, and more. What grounded me was creating a structure. I called it *The Ellavate Challenge* — a step-by-step guide to heal, reset, and grow.

I used this time to:

- *Stop people-pleasing*
- *Learn to soothe myself when emotionally overwhelmed*
- *Discover and meet my needs*
- *Have fun with myself*
- *Create a life I love*
- *Feel safe in my body*
- *Set and keep boundaries*
- *Find and pursue my dreams*
- *Learn new skills*

You stop giving love to people who cannot return it, and you pour it back into yourself. You become your own safe place.

Congratulations — you are now stepping into **Step Three!**

The next chapter will walk you through how to elevate after abuse or toxic love, day by day, with support. Let's keep going. You are doing something few people are brave enough to do.

You are coming home — to *you*.

Step 3 – The Ellavate Challenge:

This challenge is a powerful starting point if you're feeling lost or unsure of what to do next. It offers practical tools to help you reconnect with yourself and begin to elevate your life when change feels necessary.

You'll receive several weeks of structured guidance to help you heal, grow, and build healthy habits. Instead of falling into patterns like partying, swiping on Tinder, bingeing Netflix, or overworking, this challenge directs your focus back to your well-being. The goal is to care for your mind, body, and soul before addressing anything else.

This challenge has personally helped me — and many others around the world — during some of the hardest times in life. It is designed as a 66-day reset for your daily habits. The same tools you are about to explore were a lifeline for me during crisis moments. They gave me clarity, helped me build healthy habits, and supported me as I moved forward — even years after healing from PTSD caused by abuse.

Of course, there is a time and place for resting on the couch, scrolling social media or Netflix, eating comfort food, or simply checking out of life for a while. But eventually, it becomes important to notice when those habits are no longer helping.

I remember a friend asking me after a painful breakup: *"What am I supposed to do now? I feel awful. Is there something I can watch? Is there a guide to tell me what to do next?"*

I truly believe the best answers live within us. But sometimes, finding them feels out of reach. And sometimes, we avoid them on purpose. That's why this challenge exists — to guide you back to clarity and help you reconnect with your inner self.

The list on the next page includes the daily habits that form the core of this challenge. Over the next 66 days, your goal is to focus on habits that support your nervous system, strengthen your self-worth, and shift your energy from scattered to grounded.

This is not a quick fix. It is a way to rebuild from the inside out — using consistent, intentional actions that bring you back to who you truly are.

Your Daily Practices:

This challenge is a powerful starting point if you're feeling lost or unsure of what to do next. It offers practical tools to help you reconnect with yourself and begin to elevate your life when change feels necessary.

You'll receive several weeks of structured guidance to help you heal, grow, and build healthy habits. Instead of falling into patterns like partying, swiping on Tinder, bingeing Netflix, or overworking, this challenge directs your focus back to your well-being. The goal is to care for your mind, body, and soul before addressing anything else.

This challenge has personally helped me — and many others around the world — during some of the hardest times in life. It is designed as a 66-day reset for your daily habits.

The same tools you are about to explore were a lifeline for me during crisis moments. They gave me clarity, helped me build healthy habits, and supported me as I moved forward — even years after healing from PTSD caused by abuse.

Of course, there is a time and place for resting on the couch, scrolling social media or Netflix, eating comfort food, or simply checking out of life for a while. But eventually, it becomes important to notice when those habits are no longer helping.

I remember a friend asking me after a painful breakup: *"What am I supposed to do now? I feel awful. Is there something I can watch? Is there a guide to tell me what to do next?"*

I truly believe the best answers live within us. But sometimes, finding them feels out of reach. And sometimes, we avoid them on purpose. That's why this challenge exists — to guide you back to clarity and help you reconnect with your inner self.

The list on the next page includes the daily habits that form the core of this challenge. Over the next 66 days, your goal is to focus on habits that support your nervous system, strengthen your self-worth, and shift your energy from scattered to grounded.

This is not a quick fix. It is a way to rebuild from the inside out — using consistent, intentional actions that bring you back to who you truly are.

It's time to come back to yourself. It's time to Ellavate:

How to Start:

1. *Grab a journal or notebook.*
2. *Design your challenge:* What tools will support you? What feels right for you?
3. *Make a weekly plan:* Start small — add more as you grow.
4. *Track your days and reflections:* You'll be amazed at the shifts you notice.

1. Meditation:

Meditation doesn't have to look one way — there are endless ways to make it your own.

When I first began my healing journey, I spent hours in stillness, immersing myself in silence. It felt necessary, like pressing a reset button for my mind and body. Over time, I realised that shorter sessions had just as much impact. Now, my morning meditation is a non-negotiable ritual that sets the tone for a grounded, connected day.

In a world of constant notifications, opinions, and distractions, we are endlessly overstimulated. Meditation offers a much-needed pause — a chance to return to yourself beneath all the noise. For me, sitting in silence, especially in nature, is how I reset. Fresh air and open space always deepen the experience.

At first, meditation was uncomfortable. Sitting in silence felt unnatural — I would catch myself fidgeting, my body tense, my mind racing. Guided meditations helped me ease in, teaching me how to sit still without feeling restless. Even now, some days are harder than others, which is exactly why I continue the practice. The days I resist it are the days I need it most.

Everyone has their own way of meditating. Some of my friends swear by an hour-long practice, while others take quick five-minute resets throughout the day. There's no "right" way — only what works for you. Whether you need a moment of calm, a break from stress, or a way to reconnect with your body, meditation can be life-changing. Even a few minutes a day can shift your mindset and energy.

If you are new to it, start small. There are countless free resources — apps like Insight Timer and Headspace, or YouTube videos for every need. Experiment. Explore. And most importantly, enjoy the stillness. You may be surprised by what you discover in the quiet.

Your Meditation Plan:

As you begin the 66-day challenge, make meditation a consistent part of your routine.

Reflect on when and how you will fit it into your day. Will it be first thing in the morning, right before bed, or during a break at work?

Write it down and commit. The time you choose for meditation becomes your moment of stillness — your sacred reset.

2. Morning Pages:

This practice was first introduced to me during my studies as a Mindset Coach, and it resonated so deeply that I have continued using it ever since. The concept comes from Julia Cameron's *Artist's Way* method. It is simple yet profoundly impactful: first thing in the morning, grab your journal and pen, and write three pages of whatever comes to mind.

The goal isn't clarity or genius. It is not about writing something profound or even coherent.

This practice is for your eyes only. It is about releasing the subconscious clutter that weighs on your mind — emotional static that would otherwise stay stuck inside.

I like to think of it as mental and emotional housekeeping. Just as you sweep the floor or shower your body, Morning Pages cleanse your energy field and clear your mind. Most of us suppress our thoughts and emotions — this practice gives them space to breathe. By writing down your thoughts, fears, worries, and inner dialogue, you create liberation. You make room. You lighten the load. It becomes a place to process, offload, and begin your day with clarity.

Over time, I noticed something important: I was no longer dumping emotional baggage onto the people around me. I wasn't venting as much because I had already expressed what needed to come out — privately, safely, to myself.

Making Morning Pages Work for You:

Although the name implies it should be done first thing in the morning, life doesn't always allow for that. I know — especially as a parent or someone juggling multiple roles — mornings can be hectic.

If you can't do it first thing, that's okay. Find your window. Maybe it's when the children are at school, during your lunch break, or after they are asleep. The important part is making the commitment to show up for yourself daily.

This doesn't need to be perfect, but it does need to be consistent. This is your gift to yourself — a way to meet your mind where it is and gently explore what's living beneath the surface.

Enhancing Morning Pages: Add Tapping (EFT)

For an even deeper release, combine Morning Pages with EFT Tapping. After writing, read your entry aloud while tapping on your body's EFT points. This creates both mental clarity and emotional release, addressing the conscious and subconscious layers at the same time.

Try it — it's powerful.

Your Morning Pages Plan:

Reflect on when and how you will integrate this practice. Morning, afternoon, evening — what matters is that you keep your promise to yourself. Have a journal and pen ready.

Write it down. Then do it. Every day. This is your space to show up for your inner world.

3. EFT Tapping:

If you're reading this, you may already be familiar with my work. But if this is your first time, welcome to a tool that has transformed my life in many powerful ways.

EFT stands for *Emotional Freedom Technique*. It is best described as a form of acupuncture without needles. This scientifically supported method helps reduce stress and address conditions such as PTSD, anxiety, and panic attacks. In coaching, it's often used to calm emotional triggers and overcome limiting beliefs. For me, it became a deeply effective tool for regaining balance during intense moments.

As the name suggests, EFT helps you reframe your thoughts and release the negative meanings we attach to difficult emotions. In just 10–15 minutes, you can shift from panic or overwhelm to feeling more grounded and steady.

When I first heard about EFT Tapping, I wasn't sure it would work. It seemed too simple. Could something this straightforward actually help? I had only practised it as part of my coaching training, never truly relying on it.

Then came one of the darkest chapters of my life. I had just had my baby, was struggling with PTSD, and panic attacks were constant.

I was on a waitlist for therapy and felt completely lost in the rising anxiety that closed in around me.

One day, when my baby was asleep, I had a severe panic episode. I felt like I was going to collapse. My breathing became shallow, my vision darkened, and the pain in my stomach was unbearable. For the first time in my life, I thought I might need to call an ambulance. That was how out of control it felt.

And then I remembered tapping.

I didn't know exactly what I was doing, but I started anyway. I tapped, breathed deeply, and repeated simple words like: *"It is going to be okay. I love myself even when I feel anxious."*

After just one round, I felt a shift. The panic didn't escalate — it stayed still. My breath returned, my vision cleared, and the pain in my stomach eased slightly. After a few more rounds, I could think more clearly. Within 10 minutes, my breathing steadied, my heartbeat slowed, and I felt like myself again.

I was amazed. In that moment, I felt something I hadn't felt in a long time: *power*. Not from a doctor or a pill, but from my own hands. My own voice. Even now, writing this brings tears to my eyes. I hadn't realised how deeply I needed that breakthrough. I was able to calm myself — and that meant more than I can explain.

As someone who had often outsourced her self-worth and lost herself in recent years, this incident was a turning point. It showed me I was capable of handling difficult situations, of taking back control of my life, and of being a safe, steady parent for my child.

From that day on, tapping became my saviour whenever anxiety rose — and each time, it worked. I began tapping daily, on everything that surfaced.

It didn't just help with panic attacks and anxiety. Tapping helped me address deeper wounds: codependency, limiting beliefs, and low self-esteem. Over time, I became calmer, more confident, and more in tune with myself. The constant anxiety that once ruled my days began to fade.

Tapping even changed my dating life. I stopped tolerating toxic patterns and learned to walk away earlier — from addicts, narcissists, and men who used intimidation or violence. This growth expanded into every part of my life: friendships, collaborations, work opportunities. Tapping allowed me to elevate in all areas.

And it isn't just my story. A growing body of research shows that EFT Tapping is more than a "feel-good" practice. Studies demonstrate that tapping lowers cortisol (the stress hormone), supports recovery from PTSD, reduces anxiety, and even boosts the immune system.

What Is Tapping?

Tapping is based on stimulating certain pressure points while tuning into your emotions. This sends calming signals to the brain and helps reset your stress response. It breaks the loop of overthinking and allows you to see your struggles as manageable and safe.

Tapping can ease emotional intensity, release old trauma, and reduce anxiety or limiting beliefs. It reminds you to love and accept yourself — even in the mess. It offers a safe space to feel your emotions and move through them with grace.

The best part? You can do it anytime, anywhere. It's simple. It's powerful. And it works.

Making Tapping Part of Your Challenge:

There are many ways to integrate tapping:

- **Standalone sessions** when you feel triggered or overwhelmed.
- **Combined with journalling or Morning Pages.**
- **Daily maintenance** — even five minutes can reset your energy, thoughts, emotions, and stress levels.
- **Breaking through limitations** — choose one area of your life (such as self-love) for the duration of the Ellavate Challenge and tap on it.

If you're new to tapping, begin with guided EFT videos — either on YouTube or via my app. You'll find plenty of sessions to choose from; simply pick the one that feels right and follow along.

I also share my own tapping resources, including videos, scripts, and programmes, both online and in person. My EFT practice has been shaped by incredible mentors such as Brad Yates, Peta Stapleton, Gala Darling, and The Peaceful Heart Network, each of whom has helped deepen my understanding and approach.

How to Do EFT Tapping:

The simplest way to use EFT Tapping is to tap on the points and just breathe. Set a timer on your phone for 10–15 minutes. No overthinking. No special training required. Just tap and breathe.

This is perfect for stabilising your nervous system during trauma healing, when emotions feel overwhelming, or when living with PTSD. *Tap & Breathe* is the easiest way to begin. I also share *Tap & Breathe* videos on my YouTube channel that you can follow along with.

If you want to go deeper, the **Basic Tapping Process** is:

1. **Identify the Issue:**

What are you feeling right now — anxiety, grief, shame, jealousy, self-doubt? Choose one focus area.

2. **Rate the Intensity:**

On a scale of 0 to 10, how strong is the emotion? This is called your *SUD* (Subjective Units of Distress). There's no right or wrong — just your truth. This step helps you track your progress.

3. **Start Tapping:**

Use two fingers to gently tap on the following points, in order:

- Side of the hand
- Top of the head
- Between the eyebrows
- The temples
- Under the eye
- Under the nose
- Chin (under the mouth)
- Collarbone
- Side of the rib cage (under the arm)

- Wrists

4. **Speak Your Truth:**

As you tap, say statements that reflect how you feel, for example:

- *"Even though I feel anxious, I love, accept, and forgive myself."*
- *"This anxiety feels overwhelming."*
- *"It's safe to let go of this fear."*
- *"I choose peace now."*

5. **Check In:**

Pause. Breathe. Rate your emotion again. Has it shifted? If not, keep tapping. Trust the process.

This practice sends calming signals to your nervous system and reminds your brain: *It's safe to relax. We are not in danger.* Over time, tapping rewires how you respond to emotional triggers at a deep, somatic level.

The Science:

I encourage you to do your own research — you will find many studies showing how this tool affects both body and mind. EFT has been shown to:

- Reduce cortisol (the stress hormone)
- Help with PTSD and trauma
- Lower anxiety and depression
- Boost immune function

- Create observable changes in brainwave patterns

This isn't just woo-woo. It's solid neurobiology, somatic healing, and emotional freedom — all rolled into one.

Head vs. Body – The Real Breakthrough for Me:

I am a head person (hello, Virgo). I can analyse everything. I read all the books. I knew all the concepts. I understood my attachment style, my inner child, and my patterns. But I wasn't changing.

Why? Because insight alone doesn't create healing.

The real shift happened when I changed from within. When I added tapping, breathwork, EMDR, and hypnosis, I moved from simply *knowing* my trauma to actually transforming it.

Sometimes, I even had to tap before I could meditate or journal — just to overcome the resistance. That awareness itself became a tool.

Tapping and the Subconscious: Belief Rewiring:

EFT is a limiting-belief blaster. Here's how to use it:

1. **Pick a belief that's holding you back.**

- "Love isn't safe."
- "I'm not good enough."
- "I always get left."

2. **Tap on it and let the emotion rise.**

Allow yourself to feel the guilt, shame, frustration, and fear. Say it all out loud. Accept it.

3. **Use this core phrase:**

"Even though I believe this and feel this way, I love, accept, and forgive myself."

4. **Validate the emotion, then gently challenge it. Say:**

- "This belief once protected me, but I'm ready to let it go."
- "Maybe love can be safe now."
- "I choose to believe I am worthy of healthy, joyful love."

Your subconscious mind will never make you a liar — so let's tell it a better story, one you truly want to believe. Let your body feel that belief.

A friend of mine once said, **"Be careful with your self-fulfilling prophecies on love and relationships,"** after I told him what I thought my partner at the time was incapable of. I didn't understand him then. It took me another five years to grasp it. I needed to rewire my beliefs about love, and I also had to change the behaviours that grew from self-sabotage.

One belief I carried for years? That love meant pain. That if I loved, I would be hurt. So I kept love at arm's length. That belief, and the self-sabotage it triggered, ruled my dating life until I finally rewired it.

As Brad Yates says: *"Self-sabotage is just misguided self-love."*

You are not broken. You've been protecting yourself the best way you knew how. But now it's time to update the pattern.

Integrating Tapping into Your Challenge:

During this 66-day journey, choose one or two topics to focus on consistently. You can:

- Tap freestyle (speaking whatever feels true in the moment)
- Follow the scripts in this book
- Use guided videos (I've shared many on YouTube and my membership platform)

Great Topics to Tap On:

- ✓ Fear of change
- ✓ Let love in
- ✓ Love yourself
- ✓ Letting joy in
- ✓ Feeling good enough
- ✓ Releasing past trauma
- ✓ Forgiving yourself & others
- ✓ Allowing yourself to feel and heal

Tapping doesn't just help you feel better — it brings you back to yourself.

Write It Down:

- How will you integrate tapping into your life during the challenge?
- Will you tap in the morning, evening, or when triggered?
- Which topics will you focus on? (Choose no more than two for consistency.)

Have you tried my tapping app or followed my videos?

You now hold one of the most powerful emotional-regulation tools in existence. If it worked for me — and it did — I believe it can work for you. So I'll ask you: ***Are you ready to tap into your freedom and full potential?***

4. Workout – Move Your Body, Elevate Your Life:

Move your body. It doesn't need to be an intense, full-on workout every day. Rest and recovery are just as important as exertion when you're building a sustainable routine. What matters is simply moving daily — whether it's walking 10,000 steps, doing a 10–15 minute session at home, dancing in your kitchen, or trying out a new activity that gets you moving.

Regular movement is essential — not to punish your body, but to honour it. Not to change how you look, but to reconnect with how you feel.

Movement as an Act of Self-Respect:

This is not about chasing a six-pack or reshaping your body to fit society's standards. It is about choosing movement as a form of self-respect — a deep, loving decision to care for your body because you deserve to feel strong, energised, and alive.

Working out should never feel like punishment; it should feel like a gift — a sacred promise to your future self. When you show up for your body each day, even in small ways, you build a powerful kind of self-trust. You begin to feel proud, accomplished, and grounded.

Over time, that pride ripples into every part of your life — mentally, emotionally, and spiritually.

My Story: From Athletic to Abandoned to Reclaimed:

I have always been active. For as long as I can remember, movement brought me joy. I played football semi-professionally, I ran, I lifted, and I trained with friends. From my teenage years into my twenties — when I attended an elite boarding school in the US and later lived in Spain — I was surrounded by fitness-minded people. Sport and movement lit me up. They made me feel powerful, joyful, and deeply connected to my body. They made me feel good.

But then… I stopped. Not because I lost interest, but because I was criticised. My boyfriend at the time told me I was too muscular. Unfeminine.

He said I spent too much time with "meatheads" at the gym. Slowly, to avoid conflict and keep the peace, I gave it all up. I quit the gym. I quit the movement. I quit a part of myself.

My next boyfriend was jealous whenever I went to the gym. He manipulated me by saying, *"If you go, I'll go on dating apps. This is how it feels to me. You need to understand that this doesn't feel good to me."* Instead of seeing this as the glaring red flag it was, I tried to negotiate: *"What if I go to women-only gyms?"*

He found other arguments — I can't even remember them now. But the result was always the same: I didn't go to the gym. I didn't do sport. I abandoned movement — and with it, I abandoned myself.

My Commitment: Consistency Over Perfection:

During my dating sabbatical, I had a huge realisation: I missed it. I missed this part of me. I remembered the joy I felt from movement — the confidence, the post-workout glow, the mental clarity. I craved that feeling again.

It wasn't easy. As a single mum, I was exhausted. The excuses were loud. But I started small.

After giving birth to my daughter, deep in PTSD, running on no sleep, I still made one promise to myself: *move every day.* Even when it wasn't pretty. Even when it wasn't perfect. At minimum, a 15-minute workout and a walk. And I kept that promise.

It was never about one perfect workout. It was about the habit. The discipline. The devotion to my well-being. After a year, I looked back and thought: *I committed to feeling better. I showed up for myself daily. I elevated.*

That is the power of small, consistent action. One workout won't change your life. But showing up every day will. You work out for empowerment, not perfection. Recommitting to fitness wasn't about "bouncing back"—it was about coming home to myself.

It reminded me:

- I am strong.
- I can do hard things.
- I deserve to feel alive in my body.
- I show up for myself.

Movement became a celebration of what my body could do, not how it looked. It became a ritual of love, respect, and connection. That is what I want for you too.

When you move your body daily, the benefits go far beyond the physical. Exercise releases endorphins that lift your mood, ease anxiety, improve sleep, and build resilience. You may even rediscover passions or create a ritual that lasts a lifetime.

It's not about intensity — it's about showing up. Even 10 minutes matters. A walk, a stretch, a quick session on your living room floor. Just move. Your future self will thank you.

Write It Down:

- What is your movement plan for this challenge?
- What kind of workouts do you enjoy (or want to try)?
- How often will you commit to movement?
- What's your minimum baseline for days when motivation is low?

Write it down, and make it real.

5. Cold Shower – Embrace Discomfort, Build Resilience:

For years, friends raved about the benefits of cold showers. My reaction was always the same: *"No thanks!"* The idea of stepping into ice-cold water sounded insane.

Then the pandemic hit, and I began searching for ways to boost my immune system and stabilise my mental health. Once again, those same friends brought up cold exposure. This time, curiosity outweighed my resistance.

That's when I discovered the work of **Wim Hof**, a.k.a. *The Iceman*, whose breathing techniques and cold therapy methods are designed to improve immunity, energy, and resilience. With hesitation, I decided to try. That first shower was brutal. The icy water hit me and I wanted to jump straight out.

But what happened afterwards shocked me—I felt incredible. Clearer. Stronger. More alive.

Cold Showers Changed More Than My Morning Routine:

I noticed:

- My body felt stronger
- My energy skyrocketed
- My anxiety and depressive episodes eased
- My nervous system felt more balanced
- I was more resilient to stress—mentally stronger on the days I faced the cold shower

It wasn't just waking me up; it was resetting my mind and body.

At first, I found every excuse not to do it. I'd check emails, clean the house, scroll my phone—anything to avoid that freezing water. Then I saw the pattern:

Where else in my life was I avoiding discomfort?

The cold became a mirror. It showed me the places I procrastinated, avoided, or overthought. It revealed how much unnecessary drama I was creating—not just about the water, but about life.

A Mindset Shift: Resistance vs. Acceptance:

In the beginning, I used to hype myself up like a warrior: *"If I can give birth without drugs, I can do this!"* I'd shout, jump around, and psych myself up before the water even touched me.

Then one day, I stopped. I just stepped in. No mental battle. No resistance. Just… acceptance.

That small shift changed more than my mornings—it changed my approach to life. I started doing hard things without the drama, without procrastination. Just get it done—and feel powerful afterwards.

The physical and mental benefits of cold exposure are well-documented and undeniable:

- ✓ **Stronger immune system** – I rarely get sick and recover faster
- ✓ **Improved circulation** – My body adapts to temperature changes more easily
- ✓ **More energy** – Cold water wakes me up better than coffee
- ✓ **Reduced anxiety and depression** – Cold therapy helps regulate my nervous system

How to Start?

There are two simple ways to approach cold showers. Choose what feels doable for you:

1. The Cold Finish

Begin with your usual warm shower, then switch to cold water for 30–60 seconds.

2. The Full Cold Shower

Step straight into cold water. Start with 30 seconds and gradually build up to 3 minutes.

I personally prefer diving straight in. It's intense, but it wakes me up, clears my mind, and gives me an instant confidence boost.

Cold Showers as a Daily Metaphor:

What began as a way to strengthen my body has become something much deeper: a daily reminder that I can do hard things. Facing the cold every morning builds grit. It proves to me that I am resilient—that I can handle discomfort and walk away stronger.

Years later, I came across research on women's bodies, especially in relation to their cycles. Cold showers are not always beneficial at every stage. Now, with greater mental and emotional stability, I take cold showers during the phases of my cycle when they support me most. I hesitated to include this in the challenge, as it isn't a tool I use every single day. But I know it helped me through PTSD, and even now, a one-minute cold shower refreshes me and sharpens my focus in the morning.

As always, I invite you to do your own research. Listen to your body. Do what feels good for you—but don't let that become an excuse to skip a tool that has elevated me immensely.

Write It Down:

- Will you do a cold finish or a full cold shower?
- How many times per week will you commit to it during the challenge?
- What time of day will you do it?

Reflect:

- What is your cold shower revealing to you?
- Where else are you avoiding discomfort?
- Where are you procrastinating instead of simply doing the thing?

Cold showers may seem simple, but they are transformational. They meet you each morning with a question: *Will you face the uncomfortable and step in anyway?* Deep down, you already know the answer.

6. Stick to an Eating Plan – Nourish to Flourish

You are what you eat! (I mean, I haven't eaten a legend recently—but you get the point.) When you focus on elevating your body, mind, and soul, what you put into your body matters. Nutrition isn't just food—it's fuel. The way you eat directly impacts how you feel, how you think, and how you function.

We all *know* this. But here's the real question: are we actually living it?

This challenge is your invitation to take a closer look at your diet—and to begin making choices that truly support your elevation.

What Needs to Go? Are there foods, habits, or drinks you're ready to release, even just for now?

Are you thinking about eating more plant-based, cutting back on sugar, or letting go of alcohol? Maybe certain foods no longer feel good in your body, or you're simply curious about a cleaner way of living.

I realised my eating habits often mirrored whoever I was dating. If he lived on takeout, so did I. If he drank wine, I joined him. But when I was single, I naturally tuned in to what felt good—and the difference was undeniable. Clean eating gave me more energy, glowing skin, and a clearer, lighter sense of self.

Since childhood, I was naturally slim yet constantly accused of having an eating disorder. Those words left scars, and in my teens I struggled with anorexia. Later, I ate junk food I didn't even like just to "prove" I was normal. Eventually, I understood:

**ptimize*I needed to eat well, not for others, but for me.*

Now, whenever I do the Ellavate Challenge, I reset. I quit alcohol, cut sugar, sometimes remove coffee, and increase protein. Each time, my body thanks me. I feel more energised, alive, and deeply connected to myself.

What Will You Change?

On Team Ellavate, many choose to make bold shifts during this challenge:

- Going vegan or vegetarian
- Cutting out processed foods
- Starting a supplement routine
- Reducing caffeine or removing alcohol
- Trying intermittent fasting
- Actually taking those gut health or magnesium capsules sitting in the cupboard
- Quitting sugar

The point isn't perfection—it's intention. This is your time to experiment, to notice what feels good, and to discover what truly works for your body and lifestyle.

Eat to Elevate!

Healthy eating isn't about restriction. It's about freedom—freedom from old habits, emotional eating, and patterns that no longer serve you. This is your chance to create a nourishing, energising way of eating that supports the life you want to live. Not a fad. Not a crash diet. Just food that fuels you.

By the end of this challenge, you'll gain more than a new routine—you'll have a deeper understanding of how food affects your mood, energy, and overall well-being.

Write It Down:

- What will you eliminate (sugar, alcohol, gluten, etc.)?
- What will you add (vegetables, hydration, supplements, home-cooked meals)?
- How will you support yourself when cravings or triggers come up?

This is your plan. Your nourishment. Your next level. Let it reflect the self-worth you're stepping into.

7. Drink Water – A Gallon a Day!

In case you're wondering, a gallon is about four litres (3.78 to be exact). And yes—you'll be peeing a lot. But that's not a bad thing. Hydration is one of the simplest and most powerful gifts you can give your body, mind, and soul—especially while you're tapping, moving, releasing trauma, and levelling up during this challenge.

Bonus: When you're busy sipping water and making bathroom runs, you've got less time for other people's nonsense—a clear win!

My Pink Water Bottle (And What It Taught Me):

To keep myself on track, I bought a new water bottle—bright pink, sparkly, and impossible to ignore. I fill it twice a day to reach my four-litre goal, and I take it everywhere. People even tell me it inspires them to drink more water.

At first, I hesitated. *"Is this weird? Will people think it's coffee or alcohol? Will they judge me for carrying this ridiculous bottle around?"*

I almost didn't use it, just because of what others might think. I almost didn't buy it in a colour that lifted me up and made me happy, because of what others might think.

That tiny moment taught me a huge lesson: **how often do we sabotage ourselves in small ways just to avoid being "too much" or "too different"?**

I almost didn't use a simple hack that keeps me hydrated, avoids headaches, and makes me feel better—because I was too afraid of what people might think. **WOW.**

Turns out, no one thought I was weird. No one judged me. Or maybe they did, but I stopped caring. Instead, people told me they felt inspired. Now, my pink water bottle is just part of who I am. It makes life easier, keeps me hydrated, and reminds me daily: *Do what works for you, and stop overcomplicating things.*

This habit started with one simple shift: a glass of water in the morning. At the beginning of my personal development journey, I tried to change everything at once. I got overwhelmed and ended up doing nothing—on top of already being consumed by an abusive relationship. So one day, I chose just one habit: a big glass of water with freshly squeezed lemon, first thing in the morning. That single act set the tone and became an anchor. It made every other change feel possible.

During my studies in mindset coaching, I learnt hydration isn't just for physical health—it affects your entire system:

- Boosts energy
- Sharpens focus
- Aids muscle recovery
- Flushes toxins
- Keeps skin glowing
- Balances mood
- Prevents brain fog and fatigue

When you're properly hydrated, everything else flows better—literally and metaphorically.

Build your own system:

- Start your morning with one litre.
- Carry a water bottle (choose one you love).
- Add lemon, cucumber, or mint to make it enjoyable.
- Set reminders if needed.
- Track your intake—through apps, bottle markers, or even a simple journal.

And make it fun. Let your water bottle reflect you—sparkles, stickers, whatever brings a little joy to your day. These little things matter. They are what make habits stick.

Write It Down:

- How will you commit to drinking a gallon (4 litres) of water each day during the challenge?
- What system will you use?
- What time of day will you start?
- How will you track your intake?

Look Deeper: Your "Water Bottle Limitation"

Is any resistance coming up for you? Maybe you don't want to carry a big bottle. Maybe you worry you'll look "extra". Perhaps it feels strange to commit to something so simple—just for you.

Pause. Breathe. Reflect. What's your "water bottle limitation"? Where else are you holding back from something that could help or bring you joy, simply because of what others might think?

Let this be a breakthrough moment. Because how we do one thing... is how we do everything.

8. The Vortex Game

During the *In Pursuit of You* phase, I came across the teachings of Abraham Hicks, and they changed everything for me. At first, I was sceptical.

The idea of channelling a "collective consciousness" sounded far too out-there—almost like fairy-dust and feathers.

But then I listened. And later, I was hooked. Perhaps I was desperate. Perhaps I had reached such a low point that I was willing to try anything. Or maybe—just maybe—I needed that exact crisis to open a new door.

Whatever the reason, their teachings became a light. They gave me hope. They reshaped how I moved through life. As I began awakening to my patterns and inner world, I also stepped into a spiritual awakening. I explored tarot, chakra healing, Reiki, and other practices—remembering the magic I felt as a child. I reconnected to that.

What Is the Vortex Game?

The Vortex Game is a fun, simple, and powerful way to shift your energy and align your feelings with what you truly want. I first learned it from Abraham Hicks, who teaches that *"The Vortex"* is the energetic space where all your dreams and desires already exist. You don't need to "get" the Vortex—you need to align with it.

This game helps you do just that. By focusing on words that spark good feelings, you shift your state, raise your vibration, and become a match for joy, abundance, and connection—whatever it is you are calling in.

No, this isn't about toxic positivity or pretending life is fine when it isn't. It's about giving your mind and body a chance to experience the good, to rehearse the life you want to create. The truth is: we don't want "things" themselves—we want the feelings we believe they will bring. And those feelings can be accessed right now.

This mindset and emotional hack has been life-changing for me.

The Shift: From Desperate to Deliberate:

Let's say you believe you'll finally be happy once you're married. Great—let's unpack that. Ask yourself: *How do I believe I'll feel when I'm married?*

Loved. Fulfilled. Appreciated. Understood. Chosen. Like I belong.

Here's the trick: we think the thing—the marriage, the wedding day, the engagement ring—creates the feeling. But it's actually the feeling that attracts the thing. If you start cultivating those emotions now, the people, opportunities, and experiences that reflect them will begin to show up.

My "Aha" Moment with the Vortex Game:

I began playing this game during one of the darkest times of my life. I was in a toxic, emotionally abusive relationship. I didn't yet realise it was abuse—I only knew I felt awful.

During a coaching exercise, I was asked to observe my thoughts for 24 hours. The question was simple:

"If your thoughts became your reality, would your future be bright or dark?"

The answer hit hard. Within hours, I saw how negative I had become—stuck in a loop of self-doubt, fear, scarcity, and cruel self-talk. It was eye-opening.

So, I made a commitment to change. Gratitude lists helped a little, but I needed something more immediate—something to shift my energy in real time. That's when I discovered the Vortex Game.

How to Play the Vortex Game:

Start with this sentence: *"In the vortex, I feel..."*

Then, go through the alphabet and fill in words that bring you joy, love, power, or peace.

Here's an example:

A. Amazing, abundant, alive, awesome.

B. Blessed, beautiful, bold, brilliant.

C. Confident, clear, caring, creative.

D. Dynamic, daring, dazzling.

E. Empowered, enthusiastic, at ease.

F. Fabulous, flourishing, free.

G. Grateful, grounded, glowing.

H. Happy, healthy, hopeful.

I. Inspired, intentional, invincible.

J. Joyful, jubilant.

K. Kind, keen, knowledgeable.

L. Loved, limitless, luminous.

M. Magnetic, mindful, motivated.

N. Nurturing, nourished, noble.

O. Open-hearted, optimistic, outstanding.

P. Powerful, peaceful, passionate.

Q. Quick-witted, quiet-minded.

R. Radiant, resilient, remarkable.

S. Supported, successful, sexy, strong.

T. Thriving, trustworthy, tenacious.

U. Unique, unstoppable, understood.

V. Vibrant, victorious, visionary.

W. Wise, worthy, wonderful.

X. Excellent, extraordinary.

Y. Yes-minded, youthful.

Z. Zen, like a zillionaire.

You can change or add your own words, but the goal is simple: **feel the shift.** Keep going until you notice even the smallest lift inside you. Let this game be a reminder of how you want to feel—and a gentle pathway that takes you there.

Your Turn: Write It Down

Take a moment to reflect and write in your journal (or the workbook section if you've printed this book):

1. **What do you believe will make your life better once you have it?**
   Is it the relationship, the money, the house, the body, or the job?
   → Now ask: *What do I believe that will make me feel?*

2. **Which 10 words will you return to during the challenge when playing the Vortex Game?**
   Choose the ones that light you up and bring you back to your centre.

3. **How often will you commit to playing this game?**
   Set a reminder on your phone—morning and evening work beautifully, as do moments when you catch yourself spiralling into negative talk or anxiety.

4. **How can you begin to feel that desired feeling today?**
   What can you do, wear, say, or think that aligns you with that emotion?

This isn't fluff—it's neuroplasticity, energy, and habit combined in one playful tool. It's not about pretending everything is perfect. It's about choosing the next best feeling, on purpose. Let this be your practice of emotional recalibration. The more you play, the more it becomes your new normal—and from that energy, everything begins to shift.

9. Read 10 Pages a Day:

As part of this challenge, I encourage you to read at least **10 pages of a non-fiction book each day.**

Why non-fiction? Because it enriches your mind with new knowledge, fresh perspectives, and ideas you can apply straight away. Whether it's a book on personal development, emotional healing, relationships, business, spirituality, finance, or neuroscience—non-fiction keeps your brain nourished, your focus sharp, and your growth steady.

I began this habit while studying for my mindset coaching certifications in Germany and navigating the early years of motherhood. During a time of deep internal change, this simple practice gave me structure, progress, and a moment to connect with something beyond my circumstances. Just 10 pages a day kept me grounded and helped me avoid overwhelm.

Later, I used this challenge to finally finish all the books I had started but never completed—the ones I promised myself I'd read when I had "more time." Spoiler: I always had time for 10 pages. That's the magic of this habit. It's not about intensity—it's about consistency.

This part of the challenge can be whatever you need it to be:

- Finishing an educational programme you started months ago.
- Diving into a new subject you're curious about (I loved exploring Human Design, Astrology, Gene Codes, Myers-

Briggs, inner child theories, spirituality, money, and business).
- Working towards a degree, certification, or even your own manuscript

The point is: use this time to nourish your mind. Make reading a daily ritual that belongs to you.

Write it down:

- What goal are you pursuing during this challenge through reading?
- Do you want to finish a specific book or programme?
- Are you reading to support healing, growth, or purpose?
- Are you working towards completing study material or your own writing?

10. Taking Action Toward Your Dreams:

While aligning your energy and recovery habits is essential, so is taking action. During this challenge, commit to one step toward your dream every day. It doesn't need to be big or dramatic—what matters is consistency and momentum.

What is your dream?

- Start a business?
- Write a book?
- Learn a new language?
- Build a brand?
- Travel the world?

- Explore a creative passion?
- Reconnect deeply with your children?
- Try pole dancing?
- Buy a home?

Or perhaps, ask yourself: *If money wasn't an issue and no one cared what you did, how would you spend your time here on Earth?*

This is not about hustling or burning yourself out. It's about starting—taking one small step each day and letting those steps build.

I used to want instant results. I'd dive in, take massive action, and burn out (hello ADHD!). What I learned is this: real progress comes from steady, daily movement, not chaotic bursts of energy.

If you commit to this process, by the end of the challenge you'll look back and see how far you've come. You'll also gain clarity—*is this dream still right for me? Do I want to keep going?* You can't answer that without trying.

Let's be honest: *"I don't have time"* is often just an excuse. The truth is, you haven't prioritised your dream—until now.

Many people find this section of the challenge gives them the most momentum. For me, it was focusing on business growth. Others have used it to plan a long-desired trip, launch a podcast, learn a skill, or simply be more present with their children—creating rituals, play, and lasting memories.

Whatever your goal is, decide now. Then take one action each day toward it. Even something small counts—Googling how to build a website, researching family activities, or setting a meditation reminder.

Write it down:

- What dream are you committing to during this challenge?
- What small action can you take today?

Add-Ons: Make the Challenge Yours:

This is your space to personalise the challenge. Here, you can add anything specific you want to focus on—something that matches where you are in your journey. Maybe you've noticed too much screen time. Maybe you've found a new tool or practice that feels transformative. Or perhaps you simply crave more structure in your daily life.

The goal is to build a routine that reflects your values, supports your needs, and nurtures your healing. Remember: this challenge isn't one-size-fits-all. It's a framework—a strong one—but *you* decide which tools work for you. If tapping isn't your thing, that's fine. Maybe breathwork, hypnosis, or EMDR feels more effective. Use what helps. Drop what doesn't.

The focus is to steady your nervous system and step out of your comfort zone.

Some Add-Ons I've Used in Past Challenges:

- Less screen time
- Weekly breathwork sessions
- Acupuncture
- Making the bed every morning
- Magical Morning Practice (MMP)
- Hypnosis
- Journalling
- EMDR (Eye Movement Desensitisation and Reprocessing)
- Ice baths
- Acupressure mat
- Daily stretching or mobility
- Skincare routines
- Saying "yes" more often—or "no" more often
- Focusing on quality sleep
- Sauna sessions
- Anything else you know works for you

Be creative. Be intentional. Choose tools you already know lift you up.

Ask yourself:

- What do I need most in this chapter of my life?
- What have I been avoiding that I know would help me?
- What have I always wanted to try but haven't committed to?

Now is the time. This Ellavate Challenge is yours to shape. It may look different each time—and that's perfect.

Use this version to guide your next 66 days as you heal, strengthen, and elevate your life.

Write it down:

- What Add-Ons are you committing to in this challenge?
- How will you integrate them into your days with ease and intention?

The Magical Morning Practice (MMP):

A powerful practice I integrated into my life is the **Magical Morning Practice (MMP)**. Introduced to me by one of my mentors and tapping teachers, Gala Darling, this ritual is simple yet profoundly transformative.

How it works:

Each morning, you record a 2–3 minute voice note (sometimes 10–15!) and send it to a friend or accountability partner. In your message, you:

- Express gratitude.
- Set intentions for the day ahead—as if they had already happened.
- Speak about your desires—as if they had already happened.

The first step is gratitude. The key is not just to list things, but to *feel* them. This is not a mental exercise; it is a heart exercise. The more I immerse myself in gratitude, the more my energy shifts into a positive state. There is always something to be grateful for.

One of my daily gratitudes is safety—a safe country, a safe home. This sense of peace took me years to cultivate. Even now, it gives me shivers to acknowledge it, and I never take it for granted. Gratitude can be something as big as this, or as small as enjoying a new candle. The size doesn't matter—the feeling does.

Once you've anchored into gratitude, you move on to intentions and desires. Speak about your day and your future as if it has already happened. This isn't just a manifestation technique—it's a powerful shift of perspective.

For me, the MMP has been a lifeline. It helped me build trust, resilience, and deep connections during my healing after painful relationships. It also brought perspective when I needed it most. I remember venting about a disagreement with my mother. My friend replied: *"I wish I could have another fight with my mum—she's gone now."* That moment shifted everything. I began appreciating even the messy, frustrating parts of life I had once taken for granted.

The Magical Morning Practice became not only a tool for manifestation but also a practice of presence, gratitude, and emotional healing.

What MMP Has Given Me?

- A mindset shift first thing in the morning.
- A daily attitude of gratitude that flows into the rest of the day.
- A sacred space to process emotions and set intentions.
- A way to reconnect with joy and hope, even in difficult times.

If you want a morning practice that is gentle yet powerful, grounding yet energising, this is it. It is one of the simplest and most soulful ways to begin your day with clarity and positivity.

Want to try it? Choose a friend, a partner, or simply keep a private voice note journal to start your own MMP. Commit to it for one week and watch how your mindset begins to shift. It is magical—for a reason.

Acupuncture – NADA:

I absolutely love acupuncture—especially a powerful method called NADA. Originally developed to support people recovering from addiction, this form of ear acupuncture helps calm the nervous system and ease cravings. But its benefits go far beyond addiction recovery.

NADA works by stimulating specific points of the vagus nerve, which plays a major role in regulating the nervous system. By activating these points, the body is guided back into balance and calm. What amazes me is how widely this technique is used:

- In addiction treatment centres.
- As emergency relief during major disasters like 9/11 and earthquakes.
- For both victims and first responders in crisis situations.
- Psychiatric clinics.
- Counselling centres.
- Refugee centres.

While working with an NGO focused on trauma education and accessible healing methods, I had the opportunity to get certified in the NADA method. It has been life-changing—not just for others, but for me too. I now practise NADA regularly on myself, friends, and family (who often ask for it!).

The benefits speak for themselves:

- Better sleep
- A calmer mind
- A deeper sense of balance—both emotional and physical

NADA has become one of my go-to healing tools, a quiet anchor in my self-care toolkit. If you are facing anxiety, recovery, or emotional overwhelm, I truly recommend exploring this method. Sometimes the simplest tools turn out to be the most powerful—and for me, NADA has proved that again and again.

Why the Ellavate Challenge Is So Important:

I am deeply passionate about this challenge because it saved me. These steps carried me through some of the hardest and most defining chapters of my life. They weren't just habits—they were my lifeline. They shifted my mindset, broke limiting beliefs, and gave me the strength to create a life I am proud of.

I still return to the Ellavate Challenge regularly. It has become my compass, something I come back to again and again. Let's be honest—excuses are always within reach.

I had plenty, and I know you do too. That's why, once the challenge ends, there's a phase I call *integration*. This is the pause. The moment to let your body and mind adjust to your new level.

Once this new level becomes your new normal, your non-negotiable, there's space to rise again. There are always more ways to elevate. For me, that means returning to this challenge at least once a year—sometimes twice.

The question is simple: **Do you want to change your life?** Do you want to take back control—or stay stuck, clinging to the story that you are a victim of your circumstances?

Because the truth is, you get to choose. I choose to Ellavate. The fact that you are here, reading this, means you've already chosen too. Deep down, you're ready. You're ready to rise. You're ready to take action. You're ready to become the woman who leads her life with purpose and intention.

This challenge will support you whether you are in crisis or already thriving. I have done it in both seasons of my life. Each time, something incredible has emerged. I hear it from women (and men) all over the world:

"This isn't just a challenge—it's a lifestyle."

They are right. This is not a quick fix. It's a long-term shift in how you approach your mind, your body, your relationships, your energy, and your dreams.

So here's my dare to you: Take on this challenge when you feel lost—and again when you feel powerful. Because either way, it will lift you to your next level.

Step 4 – Love Yourself:

I could have made this the very first step, because loving yourself is the core of everything. It is the deep, unwavering recognition that you are worthy and whole. When you love yourself, every choice, relationship, and action flows from compassion, respect, and care. The way you feel about yourself sets the standard for how you treat yourself—and how you allow others to treat you.

For me, the concept of self-love didn't truly land until I walked away from a toxic, abusive relationship. I couldn't understand or live it while stuck in the chaos. I had to leave the abuse (Step 1), take time away from dating (Step 2), build healthy habits (Step 3), and only then was there space to discover self-love (Step 4).

Looking back, I wonder if some part of me loved myself enough to find the strength to leave. Maybe that's true for you, too. Maybe understanding self-love will be what finally gives you the courage to walk away from what no longer serves you.

Self-love looks different for everyone. I couldn't begin to practise it until I hit rock bottom. Out of desperation, I turned to spirituality and kept asking: *"What am I meant to learn from this pain?"*

The answer was always the same: *Respect yourself. Love yourself.* At first, I resisted. I thought there had to be a deeper, more profound message. But the truth circled back every time—it was this.

Eventually, I surrendered. I began researching self-love and made it the theme of my dating sabbatical. I asked myself daily: *What does it mean to love myself?* At first, it was all in my head—I understood it in theory, but not in practice.

That's when I discovered Louise Hay, whose work became a guiding light. Her words and methods gave me simple ways to start. Slowly, I noticed small changes—setting better boundaries, caring for myself more intentionally, showing up differently in daily life.

Over time, the shift became undeniable. My life was changing because I was changing—because I was finally increasing my love for myself.

True self-love is not just knowing you are enough—it is feeling it in every cell of your body. That knowing becomes your foundation. It allows you to feel safe in the world and gives you the strength to create the life you deserve.

The Uncomfortable Journey to Self-Love!

As someone who was once full of self-hate, self-loathing, and self-doubt, I can tell you—this journey was not easy. It was deeply uncomfortable.

For the longest time, I didn't even understand what it meant to "love yourself." Wasn't that automatic? My first thought was, *"Of course I love myself. But I have bigger problems—X, Y, and Z are happening in my life. How is self-love supposed to help with all of that?"*

What I didn't see then was that everything was connected to self-love. Without it, I didn't respect myself. I didn't take care of myself. I put everyone else's needs ahead of my own, constantly trying to prove my worth by doing more, giving more, being more. I was on autopilot—chasing validation, hoping someone else would fill the emptiness I carried inside.

But here's the truth: no one else can fill that void. No amount of love, approval, or validation from others will ever be enough if you don't love yourself first. I had never learned what true self-love was, and I didn't realise it was the key to everything—my healing, my growth, and my ability to elevate.

This journey meant learning to say *no*. It meant accepting that not everyone will like me—and that's still something I struggle with. It meant understanding that rejection does not define my worth. Most of all, it taught me to finally prioritise my own needs.

Raising Your Standards through Self-Love!

When You Love Yourself, Everything Changes. When you love yourself, your standards rise. What you once accepted as "normal" no longer feels acceptable. Poor treatment, toxic relationships, or unhealthy behaviours stop being tolerated, because you finally know you deserve better.

Before self-love, it's easy to normalise discomfort and disrespect. You settle without even realising how low your standards have dropped. But once you begin to love yourself, everything shifts. You stop settling—for relationships, jobs, or situations that don't honour who you are.

You start expecting more—more respect, more care, more love—from both yourself and others.

For me, self-love meant no longer accepting relationships where I was disrespected or undervalued. It meant setting boundaries, prioritising my well-being, and making choices that reflected my worth. It wasn't easy—but it was necessary.

And it doesn't stop with relationships. Self-love touches every part of life—your career, friendships, and health. You treat yourself with kindness, protect your mental and physical energy, and make choices that align with your true desires. You stop chasing approval from others because you finally know how to validate yourself.

This is why self-love is the most important step. Without it, everything else crumbles. Without it, you can't fully show up for yourself—or anyone else. But when you cultivate it, you gain safety, confidence, and a sense of control. You stop being a victim of circumstances and start leading your own life.

If you still struggle to believe in self-love, I get it. It isn't easy, especially if you've spent years in survival mode or putting everyone else first. But trust me: loving yourself is the very first step to elevating your life.

The Love Bucket:

The concept of the love bucket came to me after watching someone pour endless love into a partner who couldn't receive it. No matter how much was given, it was never enough.

That's when it clicked: love isn't just about how much is offered—it's about whether you can hold it.

Imagine this: we are all born with a love bucket, a bright vessel designed to hold the love we receive from parents, friends, partners, and the world. As babies, it overflows with unconditional love. But over time, life happens. Trauma, criticism, neglect, betrayal—they poke holes in the bucket. It rusts. The shine fades. The bottom falls out. No matter how much love is poured in, it leaks right through.

That's why you may not feel loved—not because love isn't there, but because your bucket can't hold it. You question kindness. You mistrust compliments. You reject love because deep down, you don't believe you deserve it. Even when surrounded by it, the love slips away.

Mine once looked like a dull grey tin cup, jagged and broken, with a gaping hole at the bottom. Not only could it not hold love, it could even cut the hands that tried to give it. I knew I couldn't go on like that, so I made it my mission to repair it—piece by piece, sealing cracks, polishing edges, and reinforcing the base.

Today, my bucket is vibrant fuchsia-pink with a solid foundation. It holds love. It keeps love. Most importantly, I allow it in. But this isn't a one-time fix. It requires constant care. I return to this visual often, reminding myself to pour love back into me so my bucket stays whole.

How Do You Repair the Love Bucket?

Practically speaking, repairing your love bucket means doing the mindset work to change how you see and speak to yourself.

It's about building a foundation of self-love and self-respect. It's about trusting again—believing someone when they say, "I love you," instead of doubting their intentions or only seeing the bad.

If you don't love and respect yourself, it's hard to believe others will. You might assume their love comes with strings attached, or you might not even see it at all. When your mind is clouded with self-doubt and unworthiness, love can be right in front of you and still not land. It passes straight through—like water in a bucket with no bottom. That's what I mean when I say, "The love bucket doesn't even have a foundation."

One common symptom of this is apologising for everything.

People with a broken bucket often move through life saying "sorry I exist." Instead of living in apology, begin repairing your bucket so you can hold love, receive kindness, and allow wellbeing into your life.

Exercise - Take a Moment for You:

Take a moment to close your eyes and ask yourself: **What does your love bucket look like?** Is it whole, or does it have cracks and holes? Is it full, or does it need repair?

Be honest—where are the weak spots? Rust, leaks, or sharp edges? Then imagine what it would look like if it were whole again. Strong. Radiant. Bright. What colours or details would make it reflect the love you deserve?

By visualising this, you are already beginning the repair. You don't need to fix it all at once. Start with one small act: one loving thought, one boundary, one choice to treat yourself as someone deeply worthy of love. With time, patience, and care, your bucket will hold—and keep—the love that is meant for you.

Mirror Work:

"Go do some mirror work every morning—it will help you love yourself more!" That's what my coach told me when I first began my personal development journey.

My response? *"What even is mirror work? And how is staring at myself supposed to help anything?"*

The whole concept seemed absurd. Stand in front of a mirror and talk to myself? I was sceptical, resistant, and even a little angry. I had paid good money for guidance, and this was the advice? At that stage of my life, I felt I needed something more practical.

But I had hired that coach for a reason. She was living the life I dreamed of—grounded, confident, fulfilled, and authentic. I trusted her. So, despite my doubts, I decided to follow her guidance and begin saying kind words to myself in the mirror.

What Is Mirror Work?

Mirror work is the practice of looking yourself in the eye and speaking words of love, support, and compassion. It is what you would say to a child who is hurting or a friend who needs encouragement — only now, you are saying it to yourself.

When I first stood in front of the mirror and observed my thoughts, I was shocked to realise how brutal my self-talk was:

- "You are ugly."
- "Your skin is disgusting."
- "No wonder you're single."
- "You look tired and used up."
- "You're too skinny."
- "You're too muscular."
- "You look ridiculous."
- "You can never be loved or wanted the way you look."

That inner dialogue played like a broken record, even when I wasn't in front of the mirror. Instead of offering kindness, I would beat myself up.

Worse, my mind instantly went into fixing mode:

- Buying new clothes or makeup to hide flaws.
- "Manic manifesting" from a place of desperation.
- Comparing myself to others on social media.
- Falling for every advert feeding the trap of "not enoughness."

Does any of this sound familiar? What's the first thought when you look in the mirror — and what comes after?

Once I became aware of this cycle, I knew something had to change. I began using mirror work to build a new habit: kindness.

At first, it felt strange, uncomfortable, and even wrong. Realising how unnatural it felt to say kind words to myself was the biggest shock.

But I decided to make it comfortable. To practise until I could look at myself and say something loving. That was the moment self-love finally made sense. I understood why I couldn't allow kind words or gestures from others — especially men — to land if I didn't already have them for myself.

This tied directly to my Love Bucket theory. If I couldn't hold love for myself, how could I hold it from anyone else? The messages I had heard for years — "Love and respect yourself more" — finally clicked. I made mirror work and affirmations part of my daily routine. Over time, it became normal to tell myself:

- "I love you."
- "You're doing your best."
- "You're allowed to be tired and still be worthy."
- "You're strong. You've got this."
- "I honour my feelings and allow myself to feel them."
- "I trust myself. I connect to my intuition."
- "Every day, I grow stronger, wiser, and more aligned."
- "I might not be where I want to be, but I'm not where I used to be."

The last one is my favourite. Slowly, my inner dialogue softened. The mirror became less of a battleground and more of a place to check in with myself.

Later, in my coaching sessions with traumatised women, I saw the same resistance I once felt. Many could not look themselves in the eye and say, "I love you," or "I am worth it." It takes deep inner work to get there.

So why does mirror work matter? Because when you look into your own eyes with compassion, something shifts. You finally see yourself. You meet yourself — and that's what many of us have been avoiding for far too long.

Mirror work isn't toxic positivity. It is not pretending everything is fine. It is choosing kindness, even when negative thoughts are louder. It is reclaiming your inner voice and making it your ally, not your enemy.

Standing in front of a mirror, you accept who you are in that moment while affirming that change, growth, and elevation are possible. It is simple, but transformative.

Try it. Stand in front of the mirror, look into your own eyes, and tell yourself something encouraging. It may feel awkward at first — but that's okay.

Mirror Work + Tapping = Magic:

Soon, I began adding **EFT Tapping** to my mirror work. Each morning, I looked myself in the eye, tapped through the points, and repeated affirmations like:

- "I got this."
- "I am good enough."
- "I love you."
- "I am worthy of elevating."

- "I am worthy of love."
- "I can do this."

The shift was immediate. Tapping released the inner resistance that often rises when we say affirmations we don't fully believe.

Without it, the mind screams, *"LIE!"* It feels like throwing glitter over a pile of garbage—it may sparkle for a moment, but the mess underneath still stinks.

Tapping clears that emotional clutter. It makes space for the words to land, for self-love to actually take root.

One of the most powerful phrases in EFT is: *"Even though I feel [sad/lonely/angry], I love, accept, and forgive myself."* You don't need to fake positivity.

You simply allow yourself to be where you are—and love yourself through it. That's real self-love in action.

For Moms, Kids, and Healing Hearts:

As a coach, I often see how much healing traces back to childhood wounds.

As a mother, I've come to deeply value the importance of teaching and modelling self-love to our children. When kids learn this early, they are far less likely to accept mistreatment or feel unworthy later in life.

One beautiful way to nurture this is by singing *"I Love My Body"* by Mother Moon in front of the mirror with your child:

> ♪
> "I love my body from my head to my toes
> I love my face, my eyes, my mouth, my nose
> I love the way I look when I look in the mirror
> I stand a little closer just to see a little clearer
> Who is that? It's me
> And I am looking as good as can be
> So, what do I say?
> I tell myself, I love me every day."
> ♪

Dance while you sing it. Tap while you sing. Make it playful—a morning ritual that feels silly, joyful, and healing for you and your child.

Now try it for yourself. Commit to 30 days—or even the full Ellavate Challenge—of mirror work paired with tapping. A few minutes each morning is enough. At first, you might feel resistance, sadness, or even grief. That is natural. Let the feelings rise. Healing often begins when we finally see ourselves clearly, without judgement.

And if it feels overwhelming, remember: you don't have to do it alone. Reach out to a therapist, coach, or trusted friend for support.

Self-love isn't an Instagram quote—it's a practice. Mirror work is a tool to rebuild it, one glance, one word, and one morning at a time.

Self-Love vs. Self-Care:

There was a point in my coaching journey when the word *self-love* started to feel overused—almost hollow. It had lost its meaning for me. If you feel that way too, don't dismiss it. Dive deeper. There is something there worth exploring.

For a while, I confused self-love with self-care. Because I booked spa days or got my nails done, I thought I was loving myself. But I learned an important truth: **self-care is not the same as self-love.**

Self-care is an action. Self-love is an attitude. Self-care is what you do. Self-love is how you feel about yourself while doing it. When the two meet, that's when the magic happens.

Sometimes we use self-care as a quick fix—a new outfit, a massage, a face mask. These can feel amazing, but if they only cover uncomfortable emotions, they become distractions instead of nourishment. Self-love is giving yourself permission to *be.* It is about recognising what you truly want and allowing yourself to have it—not because you earned it, not because you filled a void, but simply because you deserve it.

It means slowing down enough to feel your emotions instead of hiding behind constant doing. It is about noticing: are my actions born from love, or from fear, lack, or avoidance?

Self-love is:

- Allowing joy without guilt.
- Accepting your body, even on tired days.

- Releasing the need to prove your worth.
- Speaking to yourself with kindness and compassion.

Self-love is the foundation. Without it, self-care is hollow. With it, everything shifts. Too often we use self-care to avoid feelings we don't want to face—loneliness, anger, anxiety, and grief. We buy the dress, change our hair, get the nails done, binge-watch, swipe, scroll… and still feel empty.

That doesn't make self-care wrong. It means we need to check our intention.

Ask yourself:

- Am I doing this out of love or avoidance?
- Is this nourishing me, or numbing me?
- Am I being honest about how I feel right now?

Self-love is not something you wait for. It is a belief. A daily decision. A practice. And it is okay to ask for support—through a therapist, a coach, a group, or a trusted friend. Help is healing. You don't have to do this alone.

Self-love and Confidence:

People often ask me how I show up with confidence.

"How did you go from shrinking yourself to owning who you are?"

"How do you speak on stage, coach others, or walk into a room and own your space?"

The truth is—it's not a one-sentence answer. The answer is this book. I did the steps. I am still doing them. Every day I practise self-love and step closer to enoughness.

Confidence is a side effect of self-love.

It is not about faking it. Not about walking with your shoulders back or repeating affirmations until they finally stick. I tried that for years—it didn't work.

Real confidence came once I shifted my beliefs about myself. Once I began to feel differently about me, my confidence rose. And it still continues to grow.

I am often invited to speak and lead workshops on confidence. What I've noticed is this: even the people who *look* confident want more of it. They want it to be rooted, not performative. They want to feel it, not just show it.

The secret? **Self-love.**

Confidence is a relationship you build with yourself. Real, unshakable confidence comes when you stop betraying yourself.

When you stop putting everyone else's needs ahead of your own. When you keep the promises you make to yourself.

Every time you respect yourself, speak your truth, take up space, say no, or walk away from what isn't aligned, you build confidence. Brick by brick.

Boundaries build confidence. Healing builds confidence.

Showing up for yourself—even when it's hard—builds confidence.

Practical Ways to Love Yourself:

Now that you've learnt about self-love, you might wonder: *How do you actually love yourself?* Here are some of the most powerful, practical tools I have used—starting with the deepest one.

1. Heal Yourself:

What does it really mean to heal? Can we ever be fully healed, completely whole, and unaffected? Maybe not entirely. For me, healing is the journey of understanding the patterns we live by and the stories we tell ourselves. It's about learning to accept who you are, what you've been through, and how you've responded to life so far.

Healing means giving yourself grace for how you acted while in pain. It's recognising how past wounds show up in the present and choosing not to live on autopilot anymore.

True healing begins with awareness—knowing when you're emotionally overwhelmed or dysregulated, and learning how to soothe yourself through moments of anger, sadness, fear, or loneliness. For me, it has been about moving closer to love: with myself and with life.

One of the most powerful ways I've found to heal is by weaving self-love into everyday life. Choosing to put myself first in healthy, nurturing ways. Surrounding myself with safe people. Giving myself space to grieve.

Crying is not weakness—it's the release of energy, pain, and even old trauma from the body. Tears are sacred. They remind you of your softness and your strength.

It took me nearly a year into my healing to finally cry. I had buried my pain under layers of protection. But during a Reiki session, I let go. I sobbed. I'm not sure what exactly opened the floodgates—maybe the session, maybe life finally catching up to me—but it felt freeing. For decades I carried a hardened heart, mistrusting everyone, fending for myself, running on anger and resentment. That moment was the beginning of softening.

Healing also means letting others support you. Get a therapist. Hire a coach. Face your pain with compassion instead of fear. Allow yourself to feel. Allow yourself to rest. Allow yourself simply to be.

This is self-love. This is healing. It doesn't happen all at once, but with each broken pattern, your perspective shifts. You start seeing life differently. You become more aware. And from that awareness, you begin to evolve. To elevate.

Healing is ongoing. Just like the self-love journey, it never really ends.

The Box Analogy: Unpacking the Past

Imagine your unresolved emotions like boxes inside you. Some are taped shut from years ago. Others bulge and threaten to burst. They don't disappear. They wait—for silence, stillness, or safety.

That's why healing doesn't always feel good. When you finally slow down, those boxes rise to the surface. Big emotions may come even when you are safe or happy. That is not a setback—it is your body saying, *it's time now. Let's unpack.*

Next time strong emotions appear, ask yourself: *Is a box opening that's ready to be unpacked?*

Safety First

Healing only happens when you feel safe. Safety starts with a regulated nervous system. When you have lived through trauma, your body learns to stay on high alert—fight, flight, freeze, or fawn. Even when danger has passed, your system may still behave as if it's under threat.

A calm nervous system is vital for healing. These are some of the practices that helped me regulate mine, especially after leaving unhealthy relationships:

- Meditation
- Breathwork
- Deep rest

- EFT Tapping
- Movement and sports
- Safe relationships
- Moments of slowness
- EMDR
- Acupuncture

These practices don't just "feel nice"—they rewire you and your body. If you've noticed, the tools in the **Ellavate Challenge** are not random. There is a method to the madness. You're welcome!

2. Take Yourself on Dates:

One of the most empowering acts of self-care is going on dates with yourself.

Daydreaming about a helicopter ride over a waterfall with a partner? Why wait? Take yourself. Hesitant to dine alone at a nice restaurant because you fear judgement? That's exactly why you should.

Spending intentional time with yourself is liberating. Leave your phone behind (or tucked away) and enjoy uninterrupted you-time.

Yes, it may feel awkward at first—maybe even the whole first date—but that discomfort is a signal that you need more of it. The most important relationship you will ever have is with yourself.

If you don't enjoy your own company, you risk placing unrealistic expectations on future partners to "complete" you or make you feel fulfilled. That pressure damages relationships. Remember—we're moving beyond the need for external validation. Dating yourself is about prioritising your own company and nurturing the relationship you have with you.

Before you get to know someone else, you must know yourself. What makes you happy? What brings you peace? The more comfortable you are in your own presence, the more confident and empowered you'll feel in every area of life.

Solo dates give you the chance to fully focus on yourself—whether it's a quiet meal, a scenic walk, or an afternoon in an art gallery.

These moments help you observe your thoughts and emotions more clearly. Do you feel calm? Restless? Energised? Don't rush to distract yourself. Sit with it.

Yes, going out alone can feel intimidating, especially to places associated with couples. You may worry about what others think. But here's the truth: most people are too wrapped up in their own lives to notice—and if they do, so what? This isn't about their approval. It's about building a deeper connection with yourself.

"Those who mind don't matter and those who matter don't mind."

The origin of this quote is uncertain—Dr. Seuss, Bernard Baruch, or Alfred Adler—but its wisdom is timeless. If you struggle with people-pleasing, write it down and place it somewhere visible.

Facing this fear is an act of self-love. You're telling yourself: I am enough. I am worthy of my own time and attention. With practice, solo dates shift from awkward to natural—even enjoyable.

If you're new to dating yourself, start small. You don't need extravagance. Try one of these:

- **Go for coffee:** Take a book or journal and enjoy a quiet morning at a café.
- **Walk in nature:** Connect with yourself while soaking in fresh air and calm surroundings.
- **Visit a museum or gallery:** Explore creativity and new perspectives.
- **Treat yourself to dinner:** Try that restaurant you've been eyeing and savour the experience alone.
- **Book a spa day:** Immerse yourself in pure relaxation.
- **Join a gym or class:** Commit to movement that feels fun and energising.
- **Get witchy:** Create rituals that feel magical—tarot, crystals, astrology, or simply dancing under the moon.
- **Take a course:** Learn something new and make growth a form of play.
- **Read more:** Brew tea, find a cosy spot, and dive into a book you love.

- **Speak your love language:** Discover yours (Chapman's test helps!) and give it to yourself. Mine is quality time—so I spend it with me, guilt-free.

Solo dates are more than just activities—they deepen your self-awareness. Time alone reveals what you enjoy, what triggers you, and how you feel in different spaces. Notice your thoughts, your body's responses, and the insights that rise when you're truly present.

A side effect I loved while dating myself? Meeting inspiring women unexpectedly—conversations that left me uplifted. It reminded me that being alone doesn't mean being lonely.

The key is to **enjoy the experience, not just "get through"** it. Treat it like a real date—because it is. Dress up if you like, take yourself somewhere special, and most importantly, be fully present with yourself.

3. Discover What You Actually Love:

During my recovery from codependency, I realised something important: many of my hobbies weren't really mine. Over the years, I had picked up activities not because I loved them, but because my partners did.

In most of my relationships, I gave up parts of myself to blend into their world. Sharing interests with a partner can be beautiful, but I went too far.

Instead of trying things alongside them, I adopted their hobbies as my own and lost sight of who I was. After every breakup, I was left wondering what I truly enjoyed—and every time, I had to start from scratch.

That's why it's so important to explore what you genuinely love. Try things without pressure. Weird things. Silly things. Paint. Sing. Box. Learn to DJ. Grow herbs. Train for a triathlon. It doesn't matter whether you're good at it—what matters is noticing how it makes you feel.

The goal isn't performance. The goal is discovery.

4. Rebuild Your Love Bucket:

- What can you do to rebuild your love bucket?
- What does your love bucket look like right now?
- What would it take to restore it?
- What do you need to believe in order to feel and hold the love that's already around you?

Revisit the chapter on the love bucket and actually try the practices. Once your bucket feels whole, notice how love shows up in daily life. It doesn't have to be grand or romantic—it can be simple moments: a kind word, a smile, a friend making you dinner, a colleague bringing you coffee, someone holding the door, or even a stranger letting you go ahead in line.

Love doesn't only come from a partner. It flows through appreciation, kindness, and connection all around us. When your bucket is intact, you can finally receive it—and keep it.

5. Actions of Self-Love and Self-Care:

You can bathe in rose petals and still hate yourself. You can post affirmations and still crave external validation. The difference is intention.

Real self-love says: *"I am enough, even when I'm not doing anything. I choose this because I love myself — not to fix myself. I rest because I'm worthy — not because I'm broken."*

Self-care becomes sacred when it flows from love, not lack.

So ask yourself: What self-care can you do today that comes from love?
Maybe it's a cup of tea, a slow morning coffee, sticking to your Ellavate Challenge, a call with a friend, getting your nails done—or anything else that feels nourishing.

What's one act of self-care you can choose today purely because you love yourself?

6. Challenge Yourself to Explore New Hobbies:

If you're not sure where to start, turn it into a monthly challenge. Pick one new hobby each month and see where it takes you.

It doesn't have to be perfect or long-term—the goal is simply to explore.

You're not just filling time; you're investing in yourself. Every new activity expands your horizons, breaks old limitations, and helps you reconnect with parts of yourself that may have been lost in past relationships or painful seasons.

Write a list of things you've always wanted to try, and approach them with an open mind. Give it a chance before you judge—you might surprise yourself.

7. Pick Up Old Hobbies:

I have always loved sports. Running, hitting the gym, or taking on a new challenge—pushing myself physically makes me feel alive. It brings joy and a deep sense of accomplishment. For me, fitness isn't just about staying in shape. It's about strength, connection, and the thrill of doing something hard, whether on my own or alongside others.

At one point, I joined a military-style challenge with a group of male friends and colleagues. We were up at 5 a.m. every morning, grinding through tough workouts. After training, we went straight to work, fuelled by a strict eating plan. Evenings meant another session at the gym before collapsing into bed. We did this for three months—and I absolutely loved it. It wasn't only the physical part. It was the discipline, the camaraderie, the shared challenge. I felt like the strongest version of myself.

But the person I was dating at the time couldn't handle it. He wasn't into fitness and didn't understand how much joy it brought me. Instead of celebrating my passion, he mocked it. "You're disgusting for training so much. You're not a man," he sneered. He even ridiculed me in front of friends, calling me dumb for putting myself through "self-punishment."

His words cut deep. What once made me feel empowered started to feel embarrassing. Slowly, I pulled away from something I loved just to make him comfortable. I let my joy slide to please him.

If you've ever given up a passion to keep someone else happy, it's time to reclaim it.

Maybe you stopped because you were mocked, shamed, or made to feel small. This is your chance to take it back. See if it still lights you up.

This season—whether post-relationship or simply rediscovering yourself—is your opportunity to explore who you are without anyone's judgement. Don't waste it. This is freedom. A liberating chapter. You are no longer bound by someone else's limitations. You are free to reconnect with what makes you happy. Experiment. Play. Dive back into what once brought you joy.

8. Respond, Don't React:

"Between stimulus and response there is a space. In that space is our power to choose our response. In our response lies our growth and our freedom." — **Steven Covey**

One of the biggest wake-up calls in my healing journey was realising just how much I had tolerated. I surrounded myself with people who made me feel anxious, guilty, or ashamed—people who handed me responsibility for things that were never mine to carry.

I was the fixer. The emotional caretaker. The one who dropped everything for everyone else. People called me "loyal," "a great friend." But eventually, I reached exhaustion. I took on blame I didn't deserve. I got pulled into drama that wasn't mine. I put my own needs last, again and again, until I realised: I was being used like a doormat.

One boundary I had to learn was around availability. I had trained people to expect me all the time. Always on. Always there. And if I wasn't? I got blamed. Called "selfish." Shamed for not answering quickly enough.

The truth hit me only when I began setting boundaries: I had created this dynamic. By being constantly available, I had attracted people who thrived on taking from me. I used to apologise for replying late. I felt bad if someone was upset with me. I feared disappointing people.

Not anymore.

Now I no longer subscribe to the culture of urgency. My time, energy, and peace belong to me. Some people have access to me—but even then, I set the terms. Here's what I've learned: people who respect you will also respect your boundaries. They won't guilt-trip you or take your limits personally. The ones who do? That's your clarity—they were never safe to begin with.

I don't need to respond immediately. Not to a text, not to a comment, not online, not in real life. Not everyone needs a response. Not everything needs a reaction. Take a pause. Choose your battles. Choose your responses. That's where your power lies.

9. Boundaries As Self-Love & Self-Respect in Action:

"When you don't have boundaries, you give away your time, energy, and personal power to everyone but yourself." — **Terri Cole, *Boundary Boss***

Terri Cole is a licensed psychotherapist and author of *Boundary Boss*, a powerful guide to help people stop people-pleasing, speak their truth, and build relationships rooted in respect and authenticity. Her work, especially when combined with tapping, transformed my understanding of boundaries and my life.

For most of my life, I believed kindness meant being endlessly available. I took pride in being the one everyone could depend on. But what I called "loyalty" was often just self-abandonment in disguise.

I'll never forget cancelling both a medical appointment and an important business meeting—my own commitments—because someone I cared about was having yet another emotional meltdown. I dropped everything, believing that's what a "good" friend was supposed to do.

But that decision had long-lasting effects. Sitting in traffic afterwards, heart racing and tears in my eyes, a realisation hit me: I always put myself last. My friend thanked me, we solved her problem, and then she needed "time for herself." Meanwhile, my needs were ignored. That moment revealed a painful truth—this was the pattern in many of my relationships.

I didn't have boundaries.

Terri Cole's words echoed in my mind: boundaries are not harsh; they bring clarity. I had been giving from an empty cup, confusing over-giving with love. Somewhere deep down, I believed I was only loveable if I did more than I should.

Learning to pause, check in with myself, and stop apologising for needing space slowly changed everything. At first it felt unnatural, but over time it became second nature.

Now, I surround myself with people who honour my boundaries—some even remind me of them. When someone doesn't, I take that as information, not a personal failure.

Loving myself means protecting my energy, choosing peace, and building relationships that feel safe instead of sacrificial.

Boundaries are an act of self-love. When you set them, you send a message to the world: *I value myself.* And when you value yourself, others learn to value you too.

10. Surround Yourself with Safe People:

Healing taught me something simple but powerful: not everyone deserves access to me.

As **Mastin Kipp** reminds us, ***"The quality of your life is determined by the quality of your relationships."***

That truth struck me deeply.

For years, I was drawn to people who felt familiar. Not safe—just familiar in the way chaos had shaped my view of love. I confused intensity and drama with intimacy and depth. I thought I was being loyal, but in reality, I was abandoning myself.

Dr Gabor Maté says, *"The essence of trauma is disconnection from the self."*

He also teaches that trauma can happen in relationships, but so can healing. Healing comes with people who offer presence, compassion, and emotional safety. Safe people do not need you to perform or prove your worth.

They don't try to fix you. They honour your boundaries and make it safe to be fully human—with all your emotions, flaws, and truths. Being with them feels like finally exhaling after years of holding your breath.

Once I began to protect my peace and speak my truth, I stopped chasing connections that cost me my dignity. I started attracting people who didn't need me to shrink in order to feel loved. In that safety, I found something I didn't even know I was missing: the freedom to just be. To be worthy, whole, and at home within myself.

Creating community, building friendships, and forming meaningful connections brought a whole new level of joy into my life. Instead of looking for the next love story, I began to choose friendships that were lasting.

To be seen and valued for who you are, with all your flaws and quirks, is a gift I no longer take for granted. Being surrounded by people who don't make me feel small or anxious has changed my life. Finding safe people was—and still is—a huge part of my Ellavate journey.

11. The Energy You Allow is the Energy You Attract:

If you are always overextending, sacrificing, and giving more than you receive, you will keep attracting people who expect that. The moment you start setting boundaries, everything shifts.

You will lose people, but only the wrong ones. In their place, you will attract those who respect, honour, and value you.

I used to run toward other people's drama as if it was my responsibility. Now? I don't feel urgency. I don't absorb chaos. I listen, but I don't carry it. I stay centred. I step back. Not everything requires my energy, and not everything is mine to fix.

Boundaries are not about shutting people out. They are about protecting your peace, so that when you do show up, you show up fully and with intention.

I've also realised something else: I naturally thrive in chaos, which is why I made a career out of it. As a coach, social worker, and EFT practitioner focusing on trauma, I am surrounded by chaos daily. The difference now is that I leave it at work. I don't take it into my private life.

This became my "no drama in my private life" policy. The more I honoured it, the fewer chaotic people I attracted outside of work. Peace became the new standard—and it has stayed that way.

12. Ditching the Drama & Owning Your Growth:

Letting go of dating drama is only the first step. Once you remove toxic dynamics, you start noticing how drama shows up everywhere—friendships, family, even work.

Drama isn't always shouting matches or messy breakups. Often, it hides in gossip, constant complaining, or always being the fixer. For some, drama even provides a dopamine rush—a distraction from stillness, a way to feel needed or important.

As Tony Robbins says, *"Where focus goes, energy flows."* If your energy is constantly pulled into chaos, there's none left for healing, growth, or building the life you truly want. Louise Hay's affirmation, *"I release all drama from my life,"* captures the heart of self-love. Choosing peace over patterns isn't boring—it's brave.

Yes, people may push back. They may say, "You've changed." And they're right. Change is part of growth. You are not here to clean up after others or carry their emotional weight. Drama is not depth. Crisis is not connection.

The most loving thing you can do is step away from the noise and fully embrace your growth. And if you find yourself surrounded by drama again, pause and ask: *Do I really need to be involved—or is there a better way to spend my time and energy?*

13. Feel the Feelings:

"Grieve so you can be free to do something else." — **Nejma Nayyirah Waheed**

This line from poet Nejma Nayyirah Waheed reflects a powerful truth: feeling your emotions is not weakness—it is necessary.

In many homes, schools, and cultures focused on achievement instead of presence, we were taught to suppress, stay strong, or push through. But emotions that go unprocessed do not disappear. They stay stored in the body and show up later in relationships, choices, or outbursts.

Feeling your emotions is an act of self-respect. It means letting sadness out as tears, releasing anger through movement or sound, and meeting shame with kindness instead of judgment. We are not born fluent in emotions, but we can learn. Emotional fluency is essential to self-love. Avoiding feelings keeps us stuck, while allowing them to surface and pass makes room for healing, clarity, and growth.

If you feel sadness—cry. If you're angry—scream into a pillow, strike the ground, or move your body. When overwhelmed—breathe deeply, journal, tap, or sit in stillness until it passes. And if shame arises, respond with compassion. You don't need to understand everything right away; you only need to allow the emotion to move through.

Some ways I regulate and release emotions:

- Let yourself cry freely
- Write openly in a journal
- EFT Tapping

- Deep, intentional breathing
- Walking or gentle movement
- Screaming in a private space like a car, pillow, or in nature
- Talking to someone safe
- Wrapping yourself in a blanket or placing your hand on your heart
- Sitting quietly until the wave passes

You are not the storm. You are the one learning to stand within it—anchored in strength and grace. Emotions are part of being human. Honouring them, without judgement or the need to fix them, is one of the deepest acts of self-love.

14. Forgiveness – The Path to Freedom:

"Forgiveness is a gift you give yourself." — **Tony Robbins**

Tony Robbins, a renowned life coach and author, offers a powerful truth here. Forgiveness does not mean what happened was acceptable. It does not mean the person deserves a second chance, an explanation, or even access to your life.

Forgiveness is not about them—it is about you. It means releasing the emotional weight you've carried, sometimes for years. Many of us hold on to anger, resentment, shame, or grief because we were never taught how to let go. We wait for apologies or accountability that may never come. But if they don't, will you let your healing remain stalled?

Forgiveness is freedom. It is saying: *"I will no longer let your actions disturb my peace."*

It may feel unfair, especially when the person never admits the harm. But holding on won't make them care—it only keeps you tied to the wound. Carrying resentment is like drinking poison and expecting the other person to suffer.

Forgiveness does not excuse harm. It reclaims your energy and allows you to move forward instead of staying stuck in the past.

This also means **forgiving yourself**—for staying longer than you should have, for not knowing better, for sacrificing yourself. Self-forgiveness can be the hardest, but also the most healing. You did the best you could with the awareness you had.

Forgiveness softens your armour without taking away your strength. You don't have to be bitter to be safe. You can be wise, compassionate, and free—while still protecting your boundaries.

And remember: forgiving doesn't mean reconnecting. You can forgive and still say no. Forgiveness isn't about trusting others again—it's about trusting yourself.

Some days it will feel easier than others. That's okay. What matters is choosing peace over pain. Not because they deserve forgiveness, but because **you deserve freedom.**

As Sheleana Aiyana of *Rising Woman* writes:
"Our souls are here to grow, and sometimes that means staying longer than seems logical. But when we look back, we realize everything unfolded exactly as it was meant to."

Her words helped me forgive myself—for staying, for not knowing better, for simply being human.

Questions for Reflection:

- Who do you need to forgive—so you can free yourself? Start with one person at a time.
- What version of you do you need to forgive? Remember, you did the best you could with what you knew then.

15. Laughter – Laugh more, level up:

"Feeling good is your only job!" — **Gala Darling**

Gala Darling, author, coach, self-proclaimed "Tapping Queen," and my personal coach, lives by this mantra. Joy isn't a luxury or a reward we earn after everything else is handled—it is medicine.

Many leading voices in personal transformation agree: Louise Hay taught that choosing good-feeling thoughts is the foundation of self-love. Gabby Bernstein reminds us that when we feel good, we attract good. Abraham Hicks says simply: *"The better you feel, the more you allow."* Dr Joe Dispenza teaches that elevated emotions like joy and gratitude are key to healing and lasting change.

Joy isn't something we wait for—it's something we cultivate, especially while healing.

The Science of Joy:

Laughter reduces cortisol by nearly 32%, boosts immunity, and improves heart health. It lights up the brain's reward system, releasing dopamine, oxytocin, and serotonin—the chemicals that build resilience.

Psychologists like Dr Margaret Stuber and Dr Paul McGhee have shown that humour and laughter ease stress, help process trauma, and increase flexibility. As children, laughter and play came naturally. Somewhere along the way, we were told to "grow up," to stop being "too much." Stress, responsibility, and unprocessed pain pushed joy aside.

Reclaiming joy as adults is not immaturity—it is essential.

Joy in the Darkness:

During some of my hardest seasons, I made it a ritual to watch stand-up comedy. It didn't erase trauma, but it gave me space to breathe. That's what joy does—it makes the heavy easier to carry.

I also began noticing *glimmers*—the opposite of triggers. A glimmer is a small spark of joy: the colour fuchsia, the scent of roses, the glow of a candle, the softness of a jumper, or a song that makes your chest expand.

These tiny moments remind you that life can still feel safe and fun.

Your Turn:

So ask yourself: *What makes you feel good, even for a second?* Laughter? Colour? Music? Movement?

Whatever it is—make space for it. Prioritise it. When you feel good, you naturally attract better. Energy doesn't lie.

Make joy your daily job. Not as a performance, but as a practice. Not to ignore pain, but to remember you are allowed to feel beauty, even in the middle of it all.

How can you laugh a little more today?

16. Track Your Monthly Cycle:

Tracking your monthly cycle is a powerful act of self-love. It honours your body and recognises your rhythms as meaningful and valid. For too long, medicine and science have overlooked the female body in research, assuming we function the same every day like men. We don't—and we were never meant to.

The female hormonal cycle moves through roughly 28 days, influencing energy, mood, sensitivity, clarity, and how we connect with others.

For years, I felt embarrassed about my cycle, as if it was something to hide or excuse. That changed when I realised my emotional highs and lows were directly tied to hormonal shifts.

The Shift in Perspective:

I noticed I had more drive and confidence during the first half of the month, then became moody, anxious, or withdrawn during the second. I used to criticise myself for not being steady or consistent, pushing through and feeling frustrated when I couldn't keep up.

Over time, I learned that each phase holds a unique kind of power. The second half of the month, often dismissed as "low energy," is actually a time for reflection and reset. The anxieties and irritations that rose up were signals from my deeper self, asking for attention—not flaws to fight against.

Honouring each phase softened everything. My PMS symptoms eased. My mental health stabilised. My relationship with myself deepened.

A Dark Realisation:

I remember one of my lowest points during the luteal phase, when I felt heavy, unstable, and disconnected from my body. Depression and the aftershocks of abusive relationships already weighed me down, and the hormonal shifts intensified it all.

At that time, I tried to take my own life. The pain felt unbearable, and suicide seemed like an escape. My hormones didn't create the pain, but they magnified what I was already carrying. That experience showed me how much our cycle shapes our emotional world, and how essential it is to meet ourselves with care, not criticism.

Living in Rhythm:

Now, I plan with more awareness. I protect my energy in the second half of the month and maximise creativity and connection in the first.

The cycle has four key phases:

- **Menstruation (Inner Winter):** Rest and release.
- **Follicular (Inner Spring):** Renewed energy and motivation.
- **Ovulation (Inner Summer):** Expression, connection, visibility.
- **Luteal (Inner Autumn):** Turn inward, finish tasks, set boundaries.

Everyone's rhythm is unique. What matters is listening to your own. Track your cycle. Notice your energy, mood, and needs. Let your body guide you.

Honouring your cycle isn't indulgent—it's intelligent. And it may be one of the kindest things you ever do for yourself.

17. Praise yourself! Focus on what is right with you:

"Remember, you have been criticising yourself for years, and it hasn't worked. Try approving of yourself and see what happens." — **Louise Hay**

The shift from self-judgement to self-approval—choosing to see what is right instead of what is wrong—can be life-changing. After toxic relationships, where constant criticism becomes normal, it's easy to forget your worth. But your light is still there.

You are likely more thoughtful, creative, sensitive, and strong than you give yourself credit for. You've survived heartbreak, doubt, or setbacks, yet your courage carried you forward. Think about the traits or moments that remind you of that strength.

Praise yourself—not because you're perfect, but because you are human and learning. You don't need to keep fixing yourself. Growth comes from compassion, not criticism. You are worthy of love, exactly as you are.

Alongside self-improvement and healing, don't forget to notice what is already good in you.

Ask yourself:

- *What am I good at?*
- *What are my strengths?*

Journal on these regularly. It shifts focus from only your wounds to also your worth.

Step 5: Coming Home (To Yourself):

"Wherever you go, there you are." — **Confucius**

This quote is a reminder that your inner and outer worlds are connected. You can't shift your inner state just by changing where you live or who you're with. Your beliefs, emotions, and unresolved issues follow you until you face them.

For years, I kept searching—for belonging, safety, a person, or a purpose to anchor me. I moved homes, changed jobs, swapped routines, and relationships, hoping the next thing would finally make me happy. But wherever I landed, the same unease, the same challenges, followed me.

The shift came when I created a home for my daughter and myself—one that truly reflected us. I chose colours I loved, textures that felt good, and decorations with meaning. That space grounded me in a new way.

As I built a nurturing home outside, I began to build one within. The more I created safety and warmth for us, the more my restlessness ended.

Trauma experts say we need stability before we can process deeper wounds, and that was true for me. My home wasn't grand, but it was safe, soft, and filled with love. In that space, I could finally begin to unpack the grief, self-abandonment, and unmet needs I had carried for years.

Through self-love, nervous system regulation, and trauma work, I rediscovered pieces of myself I thought were lost—my love for tarot, pink, sparkles, meaningful conversations, movement, and laughter. These weren't trivial. They were signs of returning to myself, and my safe home made it possible.

At first, my home gave me stability. Later, I understood the deeper truth: home isn't a place—it's a feeling. It's the moment you stop waiting for the world to tell you you're worthy and begin telling yourself. You stop chasing belonging and start becoming someone you can belong to.

For me, creating a safe, peaceful home after years of abuse was one of my biggest achievements. That calm at the end of the day was something I had never known before—and I'll never take it for granted again. It's worth far more than material possessions or external success. Creating a sanctuary filled with safety, love, and laughter became a foundation for my new life.

What does coming home look like for you?

Self-Discovery Through Different Methods:

As I reconnected with myself, I also explored tools that helped me understand who I was: Myers-Briggs, Astrology, Human Design, Numerology, Gene Keys, attachment styles, and love languages. These frameworks gave me perspective and reminded me I wasn't broken—I was whole, with unique gifts, passions, and a personal blueprint.

The *Ellavate Challenge* is a space where you can explore this even more.

The Subconscious Mind – Running on Autopilot:

"Doing the same thing over and over again, expecting different results, is insanity." — **Albert Einstein**

Let's apply that to love: you can't create a new kind of relationship without addressing the beliefs and behaviours guiding your choices.

If you've found yourself repeating cycles—choosing emotionally unavailable partners, staying in unfulfilling relationships, or putting others first while losing yourself—you are not alone. You're reading this because you're ready for change.

The reason it feels hard to break free is that your subconscious is on autopilot. Without realising it, you're making choices based on old programming—beliefs formed in childhood that play out in adult relationships.

Your subconscious isn't against you. It's trying to keep you safe by repeating what feels familiar. That's why we stay in unhealthy situations: not because they're good for us, but because they feel known. But comfort doesn't always mean safety. Real healing begins when you accept that healthy love may feel unfamiliar at first. You have to train your brain and nervous system to see it as safe.

Much of this programming happened before age seven, when the subconscious was wide open. If love felt conditional or chaotic then, you may have learned to perform, stay small, or abandon your own needs.

Those strategies kept you safe as a child, but they keep you stuck as an adult.

Your patterns are not your fault—but they are your responsibility to shift. Ask yourself: Do I need to prove my worth to be loved? Do I have to give until I break? Or is there another way—one where love feels nourishing and I don't lose myself?

Your subconscious shapes most of your actions. That's why you might stay in painful relationships, ignore red flags, or fear boundaries. Deep down, your subconscious thinks this is what love looks like.

The good news is: you can rewire it. Each time you notice a reaction or a choice that doesn't serve you, pause and ask why. Why do I shrink in relationships? Why do I silence my needs? Why am I drawn to someone who withholds love? Could this be old programming?

Every time you ask, you take back power. Every time you choose differently, you interrupt the cycle and create space for something new—a love story you deserve.

Awareness creates a pause, a space between trigger and reaction. In that pause, you can choose differently. Change doesn't come from promises like "I'll start Monday" or swearing off unavailable partners. Unless you rewire the subconscious, it's like throwing glitter on a mess—it looks better for a moment, but the problem remains. Real healing begins when you clear the clutter at its source. The tools in this book—hypnosis, EMDR, and EFT—are designed for exactly that.

Exercise

1. Pause and Reflect:

The next time you feel triggered—whether it's a partner pulling away, a fear of being alone, or an urge to over-explain—pause.

Ask:

- What am I believing right now?
- What old story is playing out?

This breaks autopilot. Awareness makes the pattern harder to repeat.

2. Challenge the Belief:

Once you spot the story, question it. Is it even true?

Common beliefs include:

- "I'm not worthy unless I prove myself."
- "Love has to hurt."
- "Men always disappoint me."
- "I have to earn love."

Write it down. Ask yourself: Would I say this to a friend? If not, why am I saying it to myself? Who said this to me first? That's the root—and your chance to choose a new belief. Use EFT Tapping to anchor it.

3. **Tune into Your Body:**

Read *The Body Keeps the Score* by Bessel van der Kolk for insight into how trauma shows up physically. Your body remembers even when your mind forgets. Notice the signs—tightness, anxiety, shutdown. Movement helps shift stored trauma: shake, dance, tap, walk, or simply slow down.

4. **Create New Patterns:**

You won't rewrite your subconscious overnight, but each time you:

- Set a boundary
- Speak your needs
- Say no to chaos
- Choose peace over patterns
- Feel emotions despite discomfort
- Move your body when you want to freeze

—you're rewiring your brain. Every small step builds the foundation for healthier love.

Me, Myself, and I:

During my healing journey, especially while recovering from unhealthy love patterns and navigating PTSD, I discovered something that changed how I saw myself: I am made up of different parts that influence my decisions and shape my life. I like to think of them as three: the Inner Child (or Teenager), the Ego, and the Higher Self.

Maybe you've heard of this before, or maybe it's new to you. For me, realising that a younger part of me was still alive inside—reacting when old wounds were triggered—was one of the most healing realisations. I also came to see the ego as the part that just wants to keep me safe, and the Higher Self as the voice that knows what's truly best for me.

This framework of *Me, Myself, and I* helped me understand which part of me was speaking in each moment. Was it fear? A cry for safety or validation? Or was it the wise voice that knew I was ready to grow? Knowing who was "active" helped me respond with more love and clarity. It moved me from confusion to understanding, from abandoning myself to connecting with myself. Healing starts when we begin listening to the voices inside and choosing which one we'll follow.

Inner Child:

The Inner Child carries our earliest wounds and unmet needs. If you grew up believing love was conditional or chaotic, those messages remain in your subconscious.

When I met my Inner Child in meditation, I saw her: small, scared, longing, and left out. All the feelings I had carried into my relationships. I realised I had been living through her unmet needs, searching for rescuers instead of true partners.

But she also held joy. By reconnecting with what lit me up as a child, I began reclaiming joy alongside healing pain.

The Inner Teenager:

Our teenage selves carry wounds around identity, belonging, and love. My pattern of chasing unavailable people began here. Emotional chaos felt like love because it was familiar. My friends even told me back then, "You always go for the difficult ones."

Healing in my thirties meant grieving those early heartbreaks, releasing the shame, and offering my Inner Teen the safety and love she never had. I encourage you to do the same. Feel what's still influencing you today—the patterns end when you allow yourself to feel and heal.

The Ego:

The Ego is your survival mechanism. It clings to what's familiar, not what's good. When I began changing my patterns, my Ego panicked. It told me I was too much, too demanding, unreasonable.

But I stopped seeing the Ego as the enemy and started viewing it as a frightened protector. That shift let me respond with compassion. Every time I chose peace over chaos, I taught my Ego a new way to feel safe.

The Higher Self:

Beneath fear and survival patterns lives your Higher Self—the steady, quiet voice that knows you are already worthy.

She does not doubt. She does not control. She simply guides you toward truth and love.

Listening to my Higher Self meant pausing before reacting, choosing discomfort over dysfunction, and trusting my intuition even when I doubted. That voice grew stronger every time I chose it.

Reclaiming Your Truth:

Many of us were raised to be the "good girl"—polite, agreeable, and non-disruptive. We were taught to prioritise others' comfort, even if it meant abandoning our own truth. Showing strong emotions or questioning too much often led to shame or punishment.

If you've struggled with people-pleasing or codependency, it's not a flaw—it's programming. Seeking approval was once necessary (as a child), but as an adult it holds you back.

When you catch yourself people-pleasing now, remind yourself: *I don't have to do this anymore.* Tap on it and move on.

If parts of this book made you uncomfortable, let that discomfort be your turning point. It's a sign you are meeting the edges of old conditioning. Let it wake you. Let it guide you back to yourself.

You were not born to shrink. You were born to take up space—fully, fiercely, and freely.

Living your whole life believing you are not enough will never bring peace. It's time to rise, to stop waiting for outside approval, and to start listening to the voice within—the one asking you to elevate.

Here are three simple but powerful ways to begin reclaiming your power:

1. Stand in the Superwoman Pose.

Place your feet hip-width apart, hands on hips, chest open. Breathe deeply. Just two minutes in this posture can boost confidence and reduce stress. Bonus points if you face a mirror and speak affirmations aloud—say what you most need to hear.

2. Visualize your energy returning.

Close your eyes and imagine all the energy you've given away—to relationships, regrets, and past versions of yourself—flowing back into you. See it as light, filling and strengthening you.

3. Accept a compliment.

When someone says, *"I love your dress!"* resist the urge to brush it off with *"It's old"* or *"It was on sale."* Simply smile and say, *"Thank you."* The same goes for small acts of kindness—like when someone opens a door. Receive it graciously. Let it remind you that you are worthy.

How often do you silence yourself just to keep the peace? We say yes when we mean no. We stay quiet when we want to speak. We apologise when there's no need. All out of fear—fear of being judged, rejected, or making others uncomfortable.

Sometimes silence is wisdom. But often, silence is fear in disguise. That fear may have begun long ago. Maybe you were punished, ignored, or shamed for speaking up as a child. Maybe keeping quiet was how you survived. If so, honour that version of you. Thank her for getting you this far. But recognise that silence, which once protected you, is now holding you back.

It's time to practise your voice. Start small—set boundaries in a text, or speak out loud in front of the mirror. Say what you need. Say what's true. Bit by bit, it becomes your reality.

Affirm it until you believe it:

"I call back my power. I remember who I am. I allow myself to stand tall. I am no longer afraid to shine. I am allowed to set boundaries. I am loved when I do. I speak my truth."

With this prayer, you speak to all three parts of yourself at once—your Inner Child, your Ego, and your Higher Self. Say it. Feel it. Live it. Your voice matters.

ATTACHMENT VS. LOVE:

I used to joke that men were my strongest addiction. I could give up sugar, cigarettes, even drugs—but walking away from the wrong man felt impossible. I was confident, fun, and independent—until I fell in love. Then came the jealousy, anxiety, and neediness. I didn't recognise myself.

I'd say things like, *"I'm fine when I'm single. But in a relationship, I become someone else. Clingy. Insecure. Anxious."* And I truly believed it.

Then I discovered the concept of codependency as love addiction, and suddenly it all made sense. For years, I brushed it off—telling myself, *"I'm just loyal. I love deeply."* But after losing myself too many times, I had to face the truth.

Codependency isn't crazy or broken—it's a nervous system stuck in chaos, mistaking fear for love. As Melody Beattie wrote in *Codependent No More*:
"Codependents are reactionaries. They overreact, underreact, and rarely act. They impose guilt and feel it more than anyone else."

That landed hard for me. It gave me compassion for myself. It helped me see that I wasn't beyond repair—I just needed more love and acceptance, starting with me.

The biggest shift came when I finally understood: **love and attachment are not the same.**

- **Love** is kind, safe, and expansive. It lets you breathe. It heals. Even in hard moments, it feels steady.

- **Attachment** is rooted in fear. It clings, controls, and obsesses. It confuses chaos for passion.

When we grow up without consistent safety, we learn to associate love with anxiety, chasing, and drama. We call it passion. We call fights "normal." But it isn't love—it's survival.

ATTACHMENT STYLES: THE BLUEPRINT OF HOW YOU LOVE:

Attachment theory, developed by John Bowlby and Mary Ainsworth, shows how early emotional bonds shape adult relationships.

If your caregivers were consistent and loving, you likely developed **secure attachment**. If they were absent, inconsistent, or abusive, you may have developed **anxious**, **avoidant**, or **disorganised** attachment.

This isn't about blaming parents. Many did the best they could with what they had. It's about awareness—because awareness is where healing begins.

SECURE ATTACHMENT: THE "MYTHICAL UNICORN":

People with secure attachment are comfortable with closeness and independence. They communicate openly, trust themselves and others, and don't create unnecessary drama.

For me, they felt like rare unicorns. I dismissed secure men as boring because my nervous system was addicted to chaos. Later, I realised they weren't boring—they were safe. They were healthy. I just wasn't ready to receive it yet.

ANXIOUS ATTACHMENT: MY STORY, MY STRUGGLE:

Anxious attachment forms when love feels inconsistent. You never know if you'll be comforted or abandoned, so you overperform and cling to stay connected.

That was me. Forever chasing love, grateful just to be chosen—even by men who disrespected me. I stayed through lies, cheating, and humiliation, thinking, *"If I just love him enough, he'll change."*

But that wasn't love. That was fear. That was my childhood teaching me I had to earn love by making others comfortable.

AVOIDANT ATTACHMENT: THE MEN I DATED (AGAIN AND AGAIN):

Avoidant attachment grows when emotional needs are dismissed in childhood. These adults crave love but fear closeness. They charm you, then pull away.

I was magnetically drawn to avoidant men. Every time I grew closer, they withdrew. I mistook the push-pull cycle for chemistry when really it was my dysregulated nervous system chasing what was familiar.

DISORGANIZED ATTACHMENT: THE LOVE–PANIC SPIRAL:

Disorganised attachment mixes anxious and avoidant traits. *"I want love, but I fear it. I crave connection, but I expect betrayal."*

I lived this. I pushed love away when it was safe and clung to it when it was gone. Chaos felt like connection. Safety felt suffocating. Until I realised what I was calling "chemistry" was just dysregulation.

WHEN LOVE BECOMES AN ADDICTION: CODEPENDENCY AND THE ROOTS OF REPEATING RELATIONSHIP PAIN:

Codependency is love addiction. It's the habit of handing over your worth, identity, and safety to someone else. Not a flaw—a survival mechanism.

For me, it looked like:

- Saying yes when I wanted no.
- Taking responsibility for others' emotions.
- Staying where I was hurting.
- Abandoning dreams, friends, even parts of myself to be loved.

One metaphor that changed everything: **Milk and Coffee.**

In unhealthy love, we melt into one, losing individuality. In healthy love, coffee stays coffee and milk stays milk—separate, whole, but beautiful together.

LOVE AS A BATTLEFIELD:

Codependency isn't about caring too much—it's about losing yourself. It's staying in pain, justifying bad behaviour, and believing that if you love harder, they'll change. It's the desperate hope: *"If I do more, I won't be abandoned."*

Codependency is anxious attachment in action. It's why we stay too long, excuse too much, and ignore what we know.

I thought I loved myself—but I didn't choose myself. I still prioritised others' needs above my own. I believed:

- I'm not enough.
- Love must be earned.
- If I fix things, I'll be loved.
- Love means sacrifice.
- Being easy to handle makes me lovable.

These beliefs shaped my patterns. Healing codependency meant changing those deep inner truths and how I showed up in love.

What helped me was simple but powerful: writing down my beliefs, facing them, feeling the emotions underneath—and then rewriting them into truths that honoured me.

LETTING GO OF THE VICTIM STORY:

Letting go of victimhood was another milestone in leaving dating drama behind and elevating my love life. Yes, I was hurt. Yes, people crossed lines. Yes, it felt unfair. But staying in blame kept me stuck. Blame can feel comforting—it gives you someone to point at. But healing doesn't live there.

True freedom came when I accepted: *"What happened to me wasn't my fault—but healing it is my responsibility."*

Grieving what should have been was necessary, but I refused to let it define me. Once I told myself that staying in victim mode is boring—and felt ready for my next chapter—I could finally let go of that story.

HEALING CODEPENDENCY: THE REAL WORK:

Healing wasn't one moment. It was a journey—one that required patience and consistency. Here's what helped me step by step:

1. Acceptance and Attitude:

I stopped pretending I was fine. I allowed myself to want love and decided to heal for *me*. I admitted my insecure attachment style, even though it was hard to face. Once I accepted it, I could rise from where I was.

2. **Therapy, Coaching, and Support:**

   Sometimes I had help, sometimes I didn't. But I always sought guidance—through podcasts, tapping, mentors, and books.

   Knowing I was codependent helped me choose the right tools and teachers for the stage I was in.

3. **Nervous System Regulation:**

   I couldn't feel safe in love while my nervous system was dysregulated. So I tapped, screamed, walked, cried, breathed, and used every tool I could to calm myself. Keeping a regulated nervous system is still part of my daily routine.

4. **Rewiring Inner Beliefs:**

   I used tapping, breathwork, affirmations, hypnosis, EMDR, and inner child work to shift the beliefs keeping me stuck. I asked better questions—and gave myself better answers.

5. **Dating Detox:**

   After swinging between anxious and avoidant patterns, I stepped away from dating. I needed to feel whole on my own before trying again.

   That time gave me space to care for myself, set up my life, and raise my standards in every area—including men and dating.

Questions That Changed My Life:

- Low-level questions kept me stuck:
- Why me?
- Why am I being punished?
- What can I do to make him happy?
- Healing came with better questions:
- How did I get here?
- What beliefs brought me here?
- What am I meant to learn?
- How can I love and respect myself today?

From Self-Loathing to Self-Love:

We've already covered the importance of self-love, but let this be a gentle reminder: it's a lifelong journey. I kept hearing a quiet whisper again and again:

"You don't need to suffer to be worthy."

That whisper became a belief. That belief became a practice. And that practice turned into my new way of living.

Now, I choose myself first. I set boundaries. I don't chase. I don't beg. I don't shrink just to be loved. And if love doesn't feel safe, I no longer call it love—I call it a lesson.

My wish for you is simple: may the story of self-loathing end here, and may the journey of self-love truly begin.

Final Thoughts: This Ends With You

You are not too much. You are not broken. You are not unlovable. You've simply been patterned—and patterns can change. You're allowed to outgrow what no longer serves you, even if it once felt like home.

Healing isn't perfect, but it's powerful. And you're already in it.

So ask yourself:

- What's my attachment style?
- What beliefs am I ready to release?
- What story am I now ready to write?

What is the Imago Blueprint?

For years, I thought I had a "type": fun, witty, adventurous. But in truth, I was choosing chaos over and over again—different faces, same pattern. It wasn't preference; it was programming.

When I discovered the **Imago Blueprint**, developed by Harville Hendrix, everything clicked. The idea is simple: we subconsciously seek partners who mirror the emotional patterns of our caregivers—not to suffer, but to try and finally heal them.

We're often drawn to:

- Their positive traits (love, fun, playfulness)
- And their negative traits (emotional distance, criticism)

We chase the love we once craved, hoping this time it will be different. But instead, old wounds reopen.

Why This Matters?

The Imago Blueprint taught me something life-changing: I wasn't doomed—I was repeating. I wasn't broken—I was patterned. And once I saw it, I could choose differently.

This framework helped me heal at the root, not just the surface. It gave me clarity, helped me rewire beliefs, and showed me a new way to elevate.

The Imago Blueprint Exercise: Rewriting Your Type:

Set aside some quiet time with your journal and a warm drink. This is not about blame—it's about gentle, honest reflection.

Step 1: Identify Your Caregivers' Traits

Think about the people who raised you—parents, grandparents, or guardians.

Draw a heart-shaped diagram (or simply make two columns in your journal). Then list:

- **Top half / Left column:** Their positive traits (e.g., present, nurturing, protective, and fun).
- **Bottom half / Right column:** Their negative traits (e.g., controlling, overwhelmed, distant, critical, emotionally or physically unavailable).

Example:

- **Mother:** Nurturing, fun, present | Overwhelmed, critical, unpredictable, controlling
- **Father:** Funny, hardworking, protective | Distant, cold, emotionally and/or physically unavailable

Step 2: Reflect

Notice which of these traits show up in the people you've been drawn to in adulthood. Are you repeating the same patterns?

Step 3: Rewrite Your Blueprint

Ask yourself:

- Which of these positive traits do I want to consciously seek in my relationships?
- Which negative traits am I ready to stop normalising?
- What would a safe, healthy "type" look like for me now?

This exercise isn't about judging your caregivers—it's about breaking cycles and creating clarity. By bringing awareness to your blueprint, you begin to **repattern your love story**.

Write What You Needed as a Child:

Take a quiet moment and reflect: *What did you want to hear, feel, or receive from your caregivers that you didn't?*

Complete this sentence:

"When I was a child, what I needed most was: _____."

Examples:

- "You belong to this family. You are welcomed here."
- "I understand you. I see you. I get it."
- "You are loved and you are safe."
- "You are allowed to have fun. Life is meant to enjoy good moments."

Remember the Good:

Balance this reflection by recalling the beautiful parts of your childhood. Write down a memory where you felt happy, safe, or free—then name the feeling it gave you.

Example:

- Memory: *"Playing cards with my grandma on Sunday afternoons."*
- Feeling: *"Safe, seen, calm."*

Uncover Childhood Frustrations and Your Responses:

Now, reflect on the times your emotional needs weren't met. Write about those moments and notice how you reacted. Did you withdraw, try harder, stay quiet, or seek approval? These responses often become patterns in adulthood.

Example:

- **Frustration:** *"I felt like I didn't matter. When I wanted attention, no one listened."*

- **Response:** *"I screamed, and when I created drama, I received attention."*
  Or: *"I made the other person feel good, focusing on their needs instead of standing up for my own."*

These patterns don't just disappear—they become part of how you navigate love and relationships later, often without realising it.

Build Your Love Blueprint:

Now it's time to connect the dots. Use this framework to uncover your old "type" and see the pattern clearly:

Formula:

"I am drawn to people who are (A: negative traits), so I can try to get them to become (B: positive traits), so that I can finally feel (C: what I needed) and experience (D: the good feelings). But I often stop myself from receiving this by (E: my childhood coping strategy)."

Here's mine:

"I'm drawn to controlling, overwhelmed, critical, emotionally (or physically) unavailable men so I can get them to be present, nurturing, fun, protective, and finally make me feel chosen, safe, and like I belong. But I often sabotage that by overgiving, ignoring my own needs, or creating drama for attention."

Boom. That's the pattern. That's your old "type."

And now? You get to change it.

Rewrite Your Blueprint:

Ask yourself:

- What do I really want in a partner now?

- What emotional needs can I meet within myself?
- How can I show up as the healed version of me?

Example:

- **Old Blueprint:** "I seek distant partners to feel worthy. When an emotionally unavailable man finally chooses me, I feel like I've won—like I've proven my worth." It took me years to recognise and heal this.

- **New Blueprint:** "I choose emotionally available partners and give myself the love I once craved. Yes, triggers still surface, but instead of creating drama or pulling away, I see them for what they are—old beliefs, my hurt inner child, my fearful ego. I am in charge of how I respond. I can talk about my feelings and work through them like a mature woman, instead of reacting like the abandoned girl I once was."

Visualization: Giving It Back

This practice changed me deeply. A therapist once guided me through it, and it has stayed with me ever since.

1. Close your eyes. Picture the negative traits of your caregivers as objects placed in a box.
2. Visualise handing that box back to them—lovingly, without blame.
3. Say in your mind: *"These are yours, not mine. I return them to you with peace."*

4. Now, imagine keeping only the positive traits. Let them fill your heart like warm light.

If it feels right, write the traits on paper and then burn or release them. This ritual helped me reclaim both my power and my peace. Doing this work was like lifting a veil. I finally understood my attractions, heartbreaks, and emotional spirals. I stopped blaming myself. I stopped blaming my parents. I began to see patterns instead of failures.

That shift was everything. I went from repeating the same heartbreak with different faces to consciously choosing partners based on values, safety, and real connection. And when old patterns try to creep in? I notice them. I tap. I reset. I remind myself: *I have a choice now.*

A Gentle Reminder:

Write down your Imago Blueprint somewhere you can revisit—before a date, before you run toward that familiar spark, before you slip back into someone who feels like "home," but is really the home you fought so hard to leave.

You deserve more than the love you were taught to accept. You deserve the love you now choose to create.

Trusting Yourself:

"The antidote to uncertainty is not certainty. It is the ability to trust yourself." — **Mastin Kipp**

After toxic love ends, the silence feels unfamiliar. The chaos is gone, but doubt remains—not just about them, but about you.

Gaslighting and manipulation don't just break your heart, they break your compass. You start questioning your thoughts, your choices, even yourself. Trust in others fades, and worse, so does trust in you.

That's where I found myself—unsure of what I liked, needed, or believed. Even small choices, like picking an ice cream flavour, felt overwhelming. Years of being punished for mistakes had left me paralysed.

I had been told my reality wasn't real, my boundaries were selfish, and my needs a burden. I survived by managing others and ignoring myself. So when it was finally just me, I didn't know how to hear my own voice.

Healing is coming home. Self-trust is the door.

My self-trust didn't return overnight. It began in tiny moments—choosing what to wear without feedback, picking a book because I wanted to, and saying "no" without over-explaining. Each choice was an act of courage after years of being told I couldn't trust myself.

Underneath was fear—fear of rejection, being wrong, being blamed. But with each decision that fear loosened. I realised I could survive getting it "wrong." I could survive someone not liking me. I wasn't fragile—I was simply unpractised.

Self-trust is the foundation of elevating your love life. Without it, you give away your power, seek permission, and silence your intuition. With it, everything shifts—you spot red flags earlier, walk away faster, and choose people from alignment, not desperation.

My turning point came during pregnancy. Carrying life forced me to surrender. I couldn't rely on logic or control. I had to trust in something bigger—what I now call God, the Universe, or Source. That faith became my bridge. Even when I couldn't trust myself, I could trust that. Slowly, the external rebuilt the internal.

Let me be clear—this is not about bypassing pain. Healing requires honesty, grief, and deep emotional work. No "high vibe" mantra will shortcut the process. For me, reconnecting to spirituality through meditation, journaling, breathwork, and nature gave me the courage to hear my own voice again. It reminded me: my intuition wasn't broken. It was just buried.

Now, I no longer chase love. I don't beg people to stay. I don't micromanage life to feel safe. I trust my no. I trust my yes. I trust that even when things end, I'm still supported. Even when it hurts, I'm still held. So if you're in your version of that ice cream shop—paralysed by fear of making the wrong choice—know this: you are not broken. Start small. Rebuilding self-trust isn't about choosing perfectly. It's about choosing at all, and knowing you'll handle whatever comes next.

Trusting in the Universe was my bridge back to myself. Before I could trust me, I needed that anchor. I knew I didn't want to rely on others' opinions anymore, but I didn't yet have the confidence to trust my own. Faith gave me that start.

Gentle ways to begin:

- Choose your coffee order, your clothes, and your evening plans—without asking anyone's input. Let it be yours.
- Pause the urge to seek advice. Ask: *What do I want? What feels right to me?* Then do it.
- Be kind to yourself. You're unlearning years of programming. Be patient and compassionate.
- Connect with something bigger—God, spirituality, the Universe, nature. Let it remind you: you are not alone.
- Celebrate your wins. Every time you trust yourself—even in a small way—acknowledge it. You are building a new foundation.

This isn't just about love. It's about reclaiming the power you lost. It's about remembering who you were before fear, before the wounds, before the world told you not to trust yourself.

That version of you is still here. She's waiting for you to return.

Trust yourself. You are worth listening to.

Healing Your Trauma — The Way Back Home to Yourself:

If you've made it this far, you know unhealthy relationships aren't about "bad luck" or just picking the wrong partner. They're often shaped by deeper roots: trauma.

Attachment styles and codependency show how we relate—trauma explains why. It's where our beliefs about love, safety, and self-worth were first planted. Without healing it, we only touch the surface.

As **Dr. Gabor Maté** says:

"Trauma is not what happens to you. Trauma is what happens inside you as a result of what happens to you."

It's not the event itself—it's the impact. Trauma can be as subtle as being ignored, feeling invisible, or parenting your parents as a child. It's anything that overwhelms your nervous system and makes you disconnect from your authentic self to survive. That disconnection fuels insecure attachment and codependency.

When we disconnect, we either cling to others for identity or push them away in fear. I used to think I was drawn to "mysterious" men, but really, I was reenacting trauma. My nervous system confused chaos with love, because it felt familiar. Stable love felt unsafe, because it required trust and vulnerability.

That's what trauma does—it wires your body for survival. If love once meant walking on eggshells, peace can feel tense. If connection meant sacrifice, expressing needs can feel wrong. No dating advice can fix this. You can't think your way out—you have to feel and heal through it.

My healing began after leaving a women's shelter, grieving both the relationship and the version of myself I had lost. Small steps—many now part of the Ellavate Challenge—helped me remember my worth. In time, I became a trauma-informed coach.

Healing wasn't about fixing myself—it was about reclaiming safety, connection, compassion, and presence.

Because trauma lives in the body, healing also happens in the body. Tools like EFT Tapping, EMDR, breathwork, grounding, and gentle movement aren't just "trends." They retrain your body to feel safe, release tension, and allow rest, trust, and connection again.

"The essence of trauma is disconnection from the self. And the healing is in reconnection." — **Gabor Maté**

When safety returns to your nervous system, everything shifts. You stop chasing what hurts. You stop abandoning yourself for love. You begin to respond from wisdom instead of wounds.

One shift I'll never forget came after a breakup. Sitting in the sauna, I remembered something my coach Gala Darling once said: *"You are too hot to be sad!"* It was silly, but it reminded me I could choose to feel better. Healing didn't mean ignoring pain—I had already honored my tears. It meant deciding not to stay there.

That's what trauma healing gives us: freedom. The ability to stop fixing, proving, or pleasing—and start choosing, creating, and living in alignment with who we are. Self-love becomes the foundation. The belief that you are not enough no longer drives you. Instead, you begin from worthiness, and you elevate from there.

Step 6 – Build Your Own Life:

"Life is not about finding yourself. Life is about creating yourself." — **George Bernard Shaw**

George Bernard Shaw, the Irish playwright and social critic, spent his life challenging conventional thinking, and this quote captures a profound truth.

The Ellavate journey has guided you through rediscovery—unpacking wounds, reconnecting with your voice, and reclaiming your worth. But now comes the turning point. The next phase isn't about repairing what feels broken. It's about creating what you desire.

You are no longer the woman waiting to be handed a life. You are the one designing it. You hold the vision, the tools, and the wisdom to build a world that excites you when you wake. A life that reflects your values and honours your peace. One that feels like freedom, not survival or the endless chase for approval.

You're not here to chase life. You're here to build one so aligned with your soul that chaos and toxic patterns no longer have a place in it. This is the moment to move from asking, *"Who am I?"* to boldly declaring, *"Here's who I'm becoming."*

Your Physical Home — Building the Ground Beneath Your Feet:

For years, I said, "I just want to find home." I thought I meant a flat by the sea, the perfect city, a steady job, or a loving partner.

But no matter how many times I changed apartments, careers, or relationships, something always felt missing. It wasn't until a deep meditation in a coaching session that I heard the words: *"You are your home."* The sense of peace and belonging I longed for had to start within me, not outside.

Still, our physical space matters. It mirrors our inner world. In my twenties, my apartments looked stylish but felt empty, because I was never present. That shifted when I became a mother. Creating a home became about energy, not appearances. I wanted softness, safety, and calm—for my child and for myself. So I began with simple things: candles, flowers, warm lighting, art that lifted me. I stopped inviting drama into my space and started treating my home as a sanctuary.

I learnt how much our environment shapes the nervous system. A calm home creates safety; a chaotic one fuels stress. I'm not naturally organised, so I asked for help—from loved ones, and from professionals. I let go of the belief that I had to do it all myself.

My father once told me, "Your home is your business card." At first, I thought it meant impressing others. Now, I see it differently. Your home isn't a showroom. It's a reflection of you—a place to feel grounded, respected, and alive.

So ask yourself: How can you make your home feel more like you? It doesn't need to be perfect. It only needs to hold you, support you, and reflect the woman you are becoming.

From Self-Discovery to Self-Construction:

You've spent a season rediscovering yourself—shedding old stories, reclaiming your voice, remembering your worth. Now, the season shifts.

This chapter is not about healing the past. It is about building the future. You are no longer waiting. You are creating. This is where healing becomes action, where insight becomes structure.

Think of it like a garden: the weeds are gone, the soil is nurtured. Now it's time to plant, to grow, to bloom.

Ask yourself:

- What kind of mornings do I want to wake to?
- What rhythms feel nourishing?
- Who is the woman I am becoming?
- How does she move through her days?
- What does she believe about love, work, money, and joy?

This isn't about a five-year plan. It's about the next step, however small. Each choice is a brick in the life you're building. Let it be a life that reflects your truth. A life that feels like home.

Daring to Dream (Again):

Tony Robbins once said, *"If you talk about it, it's a dream. If you envision it, it's possible. But if you schedule it, it's real."*

At one point, dreaming wasn't allowed. You thought you had to stay small to fit in, be accepted, or be loved. This step is your permission slip to dream again—and to act on it.

The world teaches us to shrink, to be "realistic," to want less. But your soul wasn't made to play small—it came to express itself fully. Every dream is unique, yet sacred. There's no right or wrong. The only question is: *Does it feel good to you?*

We often silence our dreams because we don't know *how* to make them happen. But you don't need the how—you only need the why. The how unfolds as you do. So allow yourself to want what you want, without shame or apology. Your dreams aren't selfish. They are instructions for your path.

Many of us were told our dreams were too big, unrealistic, or out of reach. We absorbed those beliefs and settled for "safe" comfort zones. But are they truly ours—or did we inherit them from others? Ask yourself: *What if my dreams were given to me because I am capable of achieving them?*

Dreaming is not a one-off practice. It's a living journey. Your dreams may shift, and that's not failure—that's growth. In the Ellavate Challenge, one step is to take action towards those dreams, no matter how small.

Far too often, we let fear, judgement, and other people's limits stop us. We worry about not being liked, about failing, about standing out. But once you know what you truly want, go for it. Breathe deeply, allow yourself to dream big, and follow the vision that lights you up and makes your body come alive.

I once thought my dreams were too much and my story too messy. At first, I hid this book, afraid of more doubt. Some dismissed it as self-therapy, told me no one would read it, or that I should just go back to real estate. But I couldn't stop writing—I knew it mattered. Others saw it too: "You inspire people. You need to share this."

When I trained as a mindset coach, people laughed. They called it a phase, said I'd "get better" and return to "real life." But I knew this *was* my real life. And today, I know I was right to follow my dream. People across the world have told me, "I wish I'd met you sooner." A city council once said of my work, "What you and your team do is magic."

If I'd listened to the doubters, none of this would exist. I wouldn't be living a life I love or helping people the way I do. That's why I say to you now: your dream matters. Whatever it is—go after it.

Manifestation: Making Your Dreams Real:

Manifestation is bringing your desires into reality through belief, energy, and aligned action. It is not wishful thinking or controlling outcomes, but aligning your inner state with what you want so your outer world reflects it.

As Gabby Bernstein says, "The Universe responds not to what we want, but to who we are being." Wanting love, abundance, or peace is not enough—you must embody the version of yourself who already believes she is worthy of them.

Manifestation is not a one-off vision board. It is a daily exchange between belief and behaviour. You prepare for what you desire, let go of what no longer serves you, and make space for the new. You show the Universe you are ready by saying yes through your thoughts, energy, habits, and boundaries—and no through actions that don't align.

Deepak Chopra reminds us, "You must find the place inside yourself where nothing is impossible." That place exists beneath fear and beyond wounds. Desires are not random; they are guiding signals, seeds waiting to be nurtured.

You already know this truth in your love life—you've been clearing the inner chaos so unhealthy patterns no longer control you. The same principle applies everywhere. That is why the ELLAVATE Challenge is so powerful: it aligns your energy with your vision and helps you elevate your whole life.

Purpose:

In a world obsessed with hustle and performance, it's easy to confuse purpose with output. But purpose doesn't need to be loud to be powerful. It doesn't require a brand, a business, or a platform. Sometimes it's simply how you love your children, support a grieving friend, choose compassion when anger would be easier, or end toxic patterns for the sake of the next generation.

Purpose isn't always celebrated publicly, but that doesn't make it less meaningful. I never thought writing would be part of mine. I doubted it—why would my story matter? Who would care? Yet I wrote anyway, because it helped me heal. And when I shared it, women whispered, "Me too."

I never expected to work with women healing after trauma, but here I am—and I thrive in it. Clients leave my sessions saying, "I feel like a new person." That's when I began to believe in a new definition of purpose: the one that lights you up, that makes life meaningful, even if no one else understands it at first.

You are allowed to prioritise joy. To live a life that makes sense to you—not to your family, your followers, or anyone else.

Your well-being matters. When you choose peace, it ripples outward. Perhaps our purpose isn't just one thing, but two: to feel good and enjoy life, and to leave an impact—whether through kindness, compassion, raising children, ending violence, or simply lighting up a room with your presence.

Less Stress, More Freedom:

You've already survived the hardest parts. You left what was breaking you and rebuilt your sense of self. That is a rebirth. Now it's time to live differently—not harder or busier, but freer.

There is no award for exhaustion, no medal for burnout. You no longer need to stress yourself into success. The life you're building now is about peace.

Ask yourself: What would change if I truly believed I was free? What would I no longer tolerate? What would I start choosing instead?

You are free now. Free to rest. Free to breathe. Free to take up space without shrinking or apologising. One of my coaches once told me: *Ask yourself every day, how much energy do I have, and how much do I need to keep for myself?*

I often get excited about many things and overdo it. I want to be everywhere, involved in everything, until I feel overwhelmed. When that happens, I slow down. I sit in the sauna. I breathe. I pause. I remind myself I don't need to do it all in one day.

Maybe that reminder helps you too: walk a little slower when stress rises. Take a deep breath. Remember—you don't exist to survive anymore. Tune into gratitude and return to peace. You've been in survival mode for so long. Now it's time for freedom.

Self-Worth:

When I began rebuilding, I realised my self-worth was still fragile. I had learned to love myself, but trusting myself was harder. I could hold myself through pain, but could I trust myself with success?

Self-love and self-worth go hand in hand. One nurtures, the other empowers. Self-love lets you heal. Self-worth lets you rise.

Big dreams require big self-worth. If your foundation is fear or external validation, you'll sabotage what you're creating. You'll keep choosing people who treat you like an option. You'll stay in drama because deep down, you still question your value.

Confidence doesn't come first. Action does. Confidence is built by trying, failing, learning, and showing up anyway. Every time you do something you once thought you couldn't, you strengthen your inner voice. That is how self-worth grows.

Becoming the Queen of Your Queendom:

There's a lot of talk about "becoming a queen," often tied to glamour or outer power. But true queenship begins with something quieter: radical responsibility and knowing your worth.

You cannot sit on your throne while clinging to victimhood. You cannot rule your Queendom if you are waiting to be rescued or validated.

A queen doesn't beg, chase, or shape-shift to please others. She chooses. She honours her energy. She protects her peace. She knows what she will and will not accept.

For me, becoming that queen meant tough choices. Tightening my circle. Letting go of relationships that drained me, even if I still loved those people. Creating a home that felt safe and soft. Saying no as sacred protection, not punishment. Trusting that every time I chose myself, life would meet me there.

A queen doesn't need to control, prove, or perform. She is worthy already. From that truth, she builds. Her Queendom is created choice by choice, moment by moment—in how she speaks to herself, how she responds to disrespect, and how she stays rooted in her worth even when tested.

This energy transformed my dating life too. I stopped chasing men or bending to fit someone else's idea of me. I let people reveal themselves.

I stopped expecting depth from those who couldn't hold it, or hoping someone would change. Instead, I asked: *Does this person have a seat at the table I've built so carefully?*

That image grounded me. My Queendom was real. My castle was solid. My table had limited chairs, and those chairs were precious. I no longer gave them away just because someone showed interest. I welcomed people only if they brought peace, presence, and honesty.

It worked. Friendships grew deeper. The men I welcomed were healthier, more available, more caring. My standards rose. I stopped settling for crumbs. When someone didn't share my vision of the future, I walked away without convincing or clinging. Dating became clearer: Who was showing up like a King? Who was pretending? Who brought joy? Who added noise?

That is the power of living in your Queendom. You attract. You choose. No more chasing. You hold full authority over the life you're building.

A Transition into Love — The Queen Meets the King:

There is something sacred that unfolds when you stop begging to be chosen and start choosing yourself.

When you build a life that nourishes you, love is no longer a missing piece. It isn't something to chase or crave to feel whole. You are already whole. Life feels meaningful on its own. Love becomes a companion, not a lifeline. This is the shift — where conscious love begins. Not in survival or codependent need, but in expansion. Real partnership starts when you are no longer trying to fix someone, or be fixed. It is rooted in truth, clarity, and self-respect. You are not waiting for a king to rescue you. You are inviting someone into your castle who is worthy of sharing the view.

When I reached this point, I no longer wanted drama or grand gestures. I wanted peace. Emotional safety. Alignment. Someone who honoured my Queendom rather than tearing it down.

King energy feels different. It doesn't demand or confuse. It doesn't play games. It meets you where you are — in your power, your softness, your truth. This transition into love isn't about finding the perfect person. It's about being so grounded in yourself that you recognise when love is healthy — and when it's not. You stop ignoring red flags. You stop shrinking to hold interest. You stop performing.

You don't need someone to pick you. You want someone who chooses you with the same clarity and calm you've already given yourself. You don't rush. You don't force. You don't chase. You align, observe, and receive. This is love that honours the woman you've become — a love that respects your boundaries, celebrates your joy, and expands your vision instead of limiting it.

So, as you move forward — whether dating, in a relationship, or simply building your Queendom — remember this: You are not searching for love. You are creating the kind of life where love can arrive and stay.

And when it does, you'll know. Because he won't ask you to shrink. He will meet your expansion.

Step 7 – Dating:

After a certain amount of time healing and setting up your life, you are ready to build healthy relationships again. You are ready to go on dates. You don't need to be fully healed to enter love — there comes a point when connection becomes part of the journey.

We are not made to be alone. Often, we swing from codependent to hyper-independent — a defence against being hurt again. Maybe you've built safety: supportive friends, financial stability, hobbies you love. That in itself is a huge achievement after falling so low.

But remember, you picked up this book to ELLAVATE. That means stepping out of the comfort zone — not to seek drama, but because you deserve more than survival. You deserve a thriving life.

You are not looking for someone to complete or save you. You are self-aware enough now to know what you want and what hasn't worked. That is the foundation for your next step in love.

Choosing a partner is one of the most important decisions of your life. It will influence your daily rhythms, the energy in your home, how you handle stress, even the future of your children. A relationship can elevate your life — or drain it. That's why you must choose wisely.

Surround yourself with the kind of love you want. At one stage, it was essential to learn about abuse, narcissism, and codependency. But once you've grown beyond that, move on.

Don't stay stuck in bitterness or only consume content that keeps you in survival mode. Not everyone is toxic. Not every kind gesture is manipulation. Staying in that lens makes you suspicious, not selective.

If you want healthy, expansive love, start noticing it around you. Celebrate its existence instead of resenting it. When you see love in others and feel glad it exists, you align yourself with it. What you focus on grows. Where your attention goes, energy flows.

Phase one — the foundation — is done. Now it's time for phase two: going on dates, dating differently.

Phase Two – The Conscious Dating Experience:

Date differently and find a love that feels good.

Phase one is complete. Your foundation is solid. You've reconnected with your truth. Now it's time for phase two: dating in a healthy, conscious, empowered way.

That's exactly what my next sequence—**Ellavate: The Conscious Dating Experience**—is designed to help you do.

Here, you'll learn how to:

- **Go from Toxic to Thriving Love** – A bold guide for women ready to move past unhealthy relationships and step into safe, exciting, aligned love.
- **Create Your Conscious Dating Blueprint** – Practical tools, stories, and mindset shifts to date with clarity, strong boundaries, and self-trust—no more settling for mediocrity.
- **Live Your Glow-Up Era** – How to embrace single life, elevate your standards, and attract relationships that are fun, passionate, and deeply fulfilling—without losing yourself.

You are not the woman you were when you began this journey. You've survived. You've healed. You've risen. You are thriving. Now, you're ready to keep an open heart, clear vision, and a life you already love—and share it with someone who matches that energy.

Remember: **stage one cannot be skipped.** The principles in this book are your foundation. Without them, building a healthy relationship is impossible. With them, you're prepared to create love that feels good, safe, and real.

Afterthought: You Are the Blueprint

You have done what many never dare: ended the chaos, stopped the drama, and chosen yourself. *Ellavate* was never about a quick fix or waiting to be saved. It was about becoming your own anchor, stepping into your power, and remembering who you are.

You've built more than recovery—you've built the foundation of a life you love. You've reconnected to your worth and become the woman who sets the standard wherever she goes.

The beauty of this process—the shifts, the tools, the habits—is that it isn't a one-time phase. It is yours now. A guide to return to whenever life asks you to rise, whenever you need to realign, whenever you choose to expand.

This is how we lead ourselves. This is how we keep elevating—not because life is perfect, but because we are committed to building something extraordinary. And every time you choose differently, set a boundary, or say "no more," you not only change your own path—you break cycles and light the way for the women who come after you.

You have done the work. You have set the tone. Now, the woman you are becoming doesn't date as she once did. She doesn't tolerate chaos. She doesn't beg or shrink. She attracts. She chooses. She creates.

Welcome to the movement of *Ellavate*. This is only the beginning. Let's build something wonderful and lasting.

With love,
Ann-Kathrin.

The Ellavate Journal: Prompts for Self-Awareness, Healing & Expansion:

1. Morning Grounding: Start With Intention:

Set the tone for your day with presence and purpose. Ask yourself:

- What do I need today?
- How do I want to feel?
- What would support me most?
- What energy do I choose to radiate?
- What's one loving thing I can do for myself this morning?
- If today were a win, what would it look like?

2. Self-Discovery & Emotional Awareness:

- What emotions trigger me to distract myself (food, scrolling, numbing)?
- Do I seek instant validation when I'm uncomfortable?
- How do I usually respond to stress?
- Do I abandon my needs to maintain connection?
- Where do I disconnect from myself?
- Which beliefs no longer serve me?
- What am I avoiding that could help me feel better?

3. Inner Child & Emotional Roots:

Healing begins with meeting the parts of you that were never seen.

- What parts of myself did I hide as a child?
- How were my emotions or mistakes handled?
- What needs went unmet that I still seek now?
- What was valued in my family—performance or authenticity?
- What would I say to the little girl in me today?
- What did I love doing that brought pure joy?

4. Attachment Style & Codependency:

Illuminate the patterns that shaped how you love and relate.

- What does a secure relationship look like to me?
- Do I overthink or need reassurance in love?
- How do I feel when intimacy is avoided?
- Am I drawn to unavailable partners or do I push people away?
- What familiar dynamic from childhood am I replaying?
- Which attachment style best describes me?
- What 1–2 steps move me closer to secure love?

5. Love Blueprint (Imago Work):

- What traits—positive and negative—did my caregivers have?
- What emotional needs weren't met?
- What patterns link past partners to caregivers?
- How have I tried to "win" love that was missing?
- What qualities do I want in a partner now?
- What must I give myself so I stop seeking love in pain?

6. Reclaiming Your Power:

- Who am I beyond my roles?
- When did I first dim my light?
- What do I truly want but fear to claim?
- What belief about myself am I ready to release?
- What would I do if I wasn't afraid to disappoint others?

7. Forgiveness & Compassion:

- Who do I need to forgive so I can be free?
- What part of me do I still judge?
- What strength did I gain from pain?
- What fear or belief keeps me resentful?
- What would peace feel like?
- What's one step I can take toward self-forgiveness today?

8. Dating Sabbatical & Solo Clarity:

Create space to understand your motives before entering love again.

- What do I feel when I pause dating?
- Am I seeking connection or escaping?
- What does being alone bring up for me?
- What do I think love gives me that I can't give myself?
- What's one thing I've always wanted to do alone?

9. Relationship Clarity:

Questions to ask before entering (or continuing) a relationship.

- Can I grow within this relationship?
- Do I feel safe, heard, and supported?
- Are our visions aligned?
- Does my partner's behaviour match their words?
- Am I outsourcing my happiness to them?

10. Self-Love & Mirror Work:

Healing begins with the way you speak to yourself.

- What do I tell myself in the mirror?
- Am I kind or critical?
- What words do I most need to hear?
- What do I love about myself, even if unrecognised by others?
- How can I show love to myself today?

11. Healing Your Heart: The Love Bucket:

- Do I have space to receive the love I want?
- What does my love bucket look like—whole or cracked?
- What caused those cracks, and what repairs them?
- What makes me feel emotionally safe?

12. Building Your Own Life:

- What does success mean to me?
- What dream am I ready to act on this week?
- What small step can I take today?
- What lights me up—and how do I invite more in?

13. Morning & Evening Check-Ins (Daily Practice)

Morning

- How do I want to feel today?
- What do I need to give myself?
- What's one intention I can set from love?

Evening

- Where did I honour myself today?
- When did I choose peace over proving?
- What am I proud of—even if no one saw?